Are You a True Citizen of Heaven?

Are You a True Citizen of Heaven?
Copyright © 2011 by R. C. Lee

First Printing, March 2011
Printed in the United States of America

All rights reserved. No part of this book may be reproduced, stored in a retrieval system, or transmitted in any form or by any means – electronic, mechanical, photocopy, recording, or otherwise – without prior written permission of the copyright owner, except by a reviewer who wishes to quote brief passages for inclusion in a magazine, sermon or church bulletin.

Unless otherwise indicated, all Scripture quotations are taken from the King James Version.

ISBN: 978-0-9832494-4-3

In loving memory

Of

Dorothy Lee Brent

My mentor
My encourager
My precious friend

To: My valuable friend, Ho,

Your friendship has been one of my greatest treasure.

I love & appreciate you,
Chowatine

April 13, 2011

Contents

	Page
Prologue	4

A True Citizen of Heaven

Part 1   Covenant

Chapter 1   Is in Covenant with God 8

Chapter 2   Knows the Covenant God 20

Chapter 3   Must Know and Follow the Terms in the Covenant... 32

Chapter 4   Is a Part the Covenant People 36

Chapter 5   Is in Covenant with the Body of Christ 45

Part 2   Kingdom of God

Chapter 6   Intentionally Lives Under the Kingdom of God 52

Chapter 7   Feasts and Drinks at the Table of the
               Kingdom of God 60

Chapter 8   Worships God in Spirit and in Truth 70

Part 3   Divine Connection

Chapter 9   Abides in the Vine 77

Chapter 10 Returns to his/her Biblical Root 82

Covenant Prayer.. 89

Prologue

These are the "last days", perilous times. 2 Timothy 3:1-7 give a list of what men in this perilous times are like. "This know also, that in the last days perilous times shall come. For men shall be lovers of their own selves, covetous, boasters, proud, blasphemers, disobedient to parents, unthankful, unholy, Without natural affection, trucebreakers, false accusers, incontinent, fierce, despisers of those that are good, Traitors, heady, highminded, lovers of pleasures more than lovers of God; Having a form of godliness, but denying the power thereof: from such turn away. For of this sort are they which creep into houses, and lead captive silly women laden with sins, led away with divers lusts, Ever learning, and never able to come to the knowledge of the truth."

The book of 1 and 2 Timothy was written by the apostle Paul to Timothy. Timothy was the pastor of the church in Ephesus. One would hope that the list of characteristics in the foregoing paragraph be found outside the church circle but the church is plagued with such at that time and the present day. How then are we true citizens of heaven? Can we be so deceived that with such adamant expressions of ungodliness to assume that the holy God would admit us to heaven even if we have said the sinner's prayer? Is saying the sinner's prayer a passport to heaven? I trust that this book would help you to rethink and reconsider whether you are a true citizen of heaven.

These are the last days, the days of "shaking" and the days of "falling away". II Thessalonians 2:2-4, "That ye be not soon shaken in mind, or be troubled, neither by spirit, nor by word, nor by letter as from us, as that the day of Christ is at hand. Let no man deceive you by any means: for that day shall not come, except there come a falling away first, and that man of sin be revealed, the son of perdition; Who opposeth and exalteth himself above all that is called God, or that is worshipped; so that he as God sitteth in the temple of God, shewing himself that he is God".

Many scorned at the phrase, "last days", citing that the Bible has predicted the "last days" since the time of Jesus. Two thousand years have past but no sign of the "last days". However, it also means that we are nearer to the "last days" now than at Jesus' time. In any case each person has a certain time on earth before he or she dies. So in this personal context, young or old, we do not really know when our own "last days" are. We all have the notion that we will live to a ripe old age but statistics show the grim picture that many young people die before they reach adulthood.

As I wonder when this "last days" that the Bible refers to is going to happen or when my last days are, I have to rethink and reconsider whether I am a true citizen of heaven. I want to be prepared. I do not want to be amongst the list mentioned in 2 Timothy 3:1-9. I do not want to fall away. I do not want to be shaken and troubled when the shaking comes.

I trust that this book will help you to also to **take a second look at your life and evaluate if you are a true citizen of heaven.** Allow the Holy Spirit to show who you really are because the heart of men is deceitful above all things and desperately wicked (Jeremiah 17:9) and the imaginations and intent of the heart is constantly evil (Genesis 6:5). If you have not made any previous consideration to enter into covenant with God through Jesus Christ as Savior and Lord, it is my prayer that you would.

At the back of this book is a simple prayer that you can pray to enter into a covenant relationship with God through Jesus

Christ. It is not just a sinner's prayer. It is entering into a covenant with God through the blood of Jesus Christ. Before you say that prayer I would suggest you please read this book first so that you have a fuller understanding of the God of the covenant, your union with Jesus in this covenant and His kingdom.

PART 1 COVENANT

Chapter 1

A True Citizen of Heaven is in Covenant with God

Definition of the Covenant

What is the covenant? Who are the parties involved in this covenant? What has the covenant got to do with us being citizens of heaven?

Briefly, a covenant is a mutual agreement between two or more parties for a purpose. There is a promise of some sort for a specific action to be carried out or not to be carried out. So when there is a breach of the covenant, it is like a broken promise. And consequences do follow the breach or broken promise.

Unlike contracts, covenants or promises made between men, the covenant of God is made between God and man. It is divine and therefore solemn and binding. It is initiated by God Himself not by man. The covenant of God is not between equals. God and men are not equals. There is no negotiation as equals. God alone determines the terms and conditions. It is based on the sovereignty and grace of God for mankind. In the covenant of God, we did not negotiate our own salvation. We in our sinful nature and state could never attain salvation for ourselves, no matter how hard we try. Salvation was initiated by God because of His love for us. Without this act of God, we will be eternally lost, faced with the grim future of eternal death.

Even though the covenant of God is initiated by God Himself, this covenant is two-sided. God initiated the covenant but we have to make a response. Let us take a look at two examples from the Old Testament; the covenant that God made with Abraham and the covenant He made with David.

The Old Covenant of God
a) God's Covenant with Abraham

Genesis chapter 12 records God speaking to Abraham for the first time and making promises to Abraham. God initiated the promises to Abraham. Tradition indicates that Abraham's family background was idol worship. They may have known a little bit about the Lord God and may have worshipped Him as one of their deities but definitely did not know the Lord God personally.

Genesis 12:1-4
1 Now <u>the LORD had said unto Abram</u>, Get thee out of thy country, and from thy kindred, and from thy father's house, unto a land that I will shew thee:
2 And I will make of thee a great nation, and I will bless thee, and make thy name great; and thou shalt be a blessing:
3 And I will bless them that bless thee, and curse him that curseth thee: and in thee shall all families of the earth be blessed.
4 So Abram departed, as the LORD had spoken unto him; and Lot went with him: and Abram was seventy and five years old when he departed out of Haran.

God told Abraham to leave his country and family and go to a land which He will show him. We see in verse 1 that God initiated the calling. Abraham responded to God and did as the Lord God told him to. By his response to God; leaving his country and his family, taking only his wife, Sarah, and his nephew, Lot, along with their servants and possessions, Abraham accepted the covenant and separated himself unto God. Thus, begun Abraham's journey of faith and communion with God. His walk with God was so close that he alone was called "the friend of God" in the bible (2 Chronicles 20:7, "Art not thou our God, who didst drive out the inhabitants of this land before thy people Israel, and gavest it to the seed of Abraham thy friend for ever?).

In Genesis 15:6, it is stated that Abraham "believed in the LORD; and he counted it to him for righteousness." His response to God based on faith, afforded him to be one of the faith heroes recorded in Hebrews chapter 11.

Hebrews 11:8-10

8 <u>By faith</u> Abraham, when he was <u>called to go</u> out into a place which he should after receive for an inheritance, <u>obeyed</u>; and he went out, not knowing whither he went.

9 <u>By faith</u> he sojourned in the land of promise, as in a strange country, dwelling in tabernacles with Isaac and Jacob, the heirs with him of the same promise:

10 For he looked for a city which hath foundations, whose builder and maker is God.

From Genesis chapter 12 to chapter 16, we see God making promises to Abraham. We did not see much of God's requirement of Abraham's part in the covenant until Genesis chapter 17.

Genesis 17:1-9

1 And when Abram was ninety years old and nine, the LORD appeared to Abram, and said unto him, I am the Almighty God; <u>walk before me, and be thou perfect</u>.

2 And I will make my covenant between me and thee, and <u>will multiply thee exceedingly</u>.

3 And Abram fell on his face: and God talked with him, saying,

4 As for me, behold, my covenant is with thee, and <u>thou shalt be a father of many nations</u>.

5 Neither shall thy name any more be called Abram, but thy name shall be Abraham; for a father of many nations have I made thee.

6 And I <u>will make thee exceeding fruitful</u>, and I <u>will make nations of thee</u>, and <u>kings shall come out of thee</u>.

7 And I <u>will establish my covenant between me and thee</u> and thy seed after thee in their generations <u>for an everlasting covenant</u>, to be a God unto thee, and to thy seed after thee.

8 And I <u>will give unto thee, and to thy seed after thee, the land</u> wherein thou art a stranger, all the land of Canaan, for <u>an everlasting possession</u>; and I <u>will be their God</u>.

9 And God said unto Abraham, Thou <u>shalt keep my covenant therefore, thou, and thy seed after thee in their generations</u>.

From the foregoing passage we see these requirements on Abraham's part: "<u>walk before me, and be thou perfect</u>" (verse 1); "keep my covenant ... thou and thy seed after thee in their generations" (verse 9). These requirements upon Abraham seem little compared to the promises that God would do on His part. God "will multiply him exceedingly" (verse 2); make him "a father of many nations" (verse 4, 6); "make him exceedingly fruitful" (verse 6); "establish an everlasting covenant with him and his descendants" (verse 7); "give him and his descendants the land where they are strangers as an everlasting possession"; and "will be their God" (verse 8).

Did Abraham's journey and walk with God end when he died? Hebrews 11:13-16 indicates that it did not end when he died. It continued to a heavenly country.

13 These all died in faith, not having received the promises, but having seen them afar off, and were persuaded of them, and embraced them, and confessed that they were strangers and pilgrims on the earth.
14 For they that say such things declare plainly that they seek a country.
15 And truly, if they had been mindful of that country from whence they came out, they might have had opportunity to have returned.
16 But now they <u>desire a better country</u>, that is, an <u>heavenly</u>: wherefore God is not ashamed to be called their <u>God: for he hath prepared for them a city</u>.

How is the covenant of Abraham applicable to us today? Galatians 3:14 "That the blessing of Abraham might come on the Gentiles through Jesus Christ; that we might receive the promise of the Spirit through faith." Then in verse 29 it says, "And if you are Christ's; then you are Abraham's seed, and heirs according to the promises."

b) <u>God's Covenant with David</u>

David was the youngest son and a shepherd, relatively insignificant by man's standard and would have been by-passed by both his father, Jesse, and the prophet, Samuel, had it not been the intervention of God.

1 Samuel 16:1-13

1 And the LORD said unto Samuel, How long wilt thou mourn for Saul, seeing I have rejected him from reigning over Israel? fill thine horn with oil, and go, I will send thee to Jesse the Bethlehemite: for I have provided me a king among his sons.

2 And Samuel said, How can I go? if Saul hear it, he will kill me. And the LORD said, Take an heifer with thee, and say, I am come to sacrifice to the LORD.

3 And call Jesse to the sacrifice, and I will shew thee what thou shalt do: and thou shalt anoint unto me him whom I name unto thee.

4 And Samuel did that which the LORD spake, and came to Bethlehem. And the elders of the town trembled at his coming, and said, Comest thou peaceably?

5 And he said, Peaceably: I am come to sacrifice unto the LORD: sanctify yourselves, and come with me to the sacrifice. And he sanctified Jesse and his sons, and called them to the sacrifice.

6 And it came to pass, when they were come, that he looked on Eliab, and said, Surely the LORD's anointed is before him.

7 But the LORD said unto Samuel, Look not on his countenance, or on the height of his stature; because I have refused him: for the LORD seeth not as man seeth; for man looketh on the outward appearance, but the LORD looketh on the heart.

8 Then Jesse called Abinadab, and made him pass before Samuel. And he said, Neither hath the LORD chosen this.

9 Then Jesse made Shammah to pass by. And he said, Neither hath the LORD chosen this.

10 Again, Jesse made seven of his sons to pass before Samuel. And Samuel said unto Jesse, The LORD hath not chosen these.

11 And Samuel said unto Jesse, Are here all thy children? And he said, There remaineth yet the youngest, and, behold, he keepeth the sheep. And Samuel said unto Jesse, Send and fetch him: for we will not sit down till he come hither.

12 And he sent, and brought him in. Now he was ruddy, and withal of a beautiful countenance, and goodly to look to. And the LORD said, Arise, anoint him: for this is he.

13 Then Samuel took the horn of oil, and anointed him in the midst of his brethren: and the Spirit of the LORD came upon David from that day forward. So Samuel rose up, and went to Ramah.

Here, again, we see that God initiated the calling of David. David was just minding sheep when God singled him out (2 Samuel 7:8). But we know from the Psalms David wrote, such as Psalm 23, that he, unlike Abraham, already knew God in a personal way. David responded to God by humbling and submitting himself before God's prophet, Samuel. He allowed Samuel to anoint him with oil, knowing full well what that symbolic act meant. David's separation unto God was further strengthened when the Spirit of the Lord came upon him when he was anointed by Samuel.

From this point onwards we see how God began to open the way for David to experience life in the king's palace. It started with David being sent for, to play the harp for King Saul. Whenever Saul was distressed, David's music would sooth Saul and he became well (1 Samuel 16:23). Saul made David his armor bearer (1 Samuel 16: 21). Saul even gave his daughter, Michal, as wife to David (1 Samuel 17:27). It was God's plan to make David king over His people. But the ultimate plan was to establish an everlasting kingdom in Jesus Christ through David.

Jeremiah 23:5-6

5 Behold, the days come, saith the LORD, that I will raise unto David a righteous Branch, and a King shall reign and prosper, and shall execute judgment and justice in the earth.

6 In his days Judah shall be saved, and Israel shall dwell safely: and this is his name whereby he shall be called, THE LORD OUR RIGHTEOUSNESS.

Jesus himself declared in Revelation 22:16, "I Jesus have sent mine angel to testify unto you these things in the churches. I am the root and the offspring of David, and the bright and morning star."

The promises of the covenant of God with David are laid out clearly in 2 Samuel 7:8-16.

8 Now therefore so shalt thou say unto my servant David, Thus saith the LORD of hosts, I took thee from the sheepcote, from following the sheep, to be ruler over my people, over Israel:

9 And I was <u>with thee whithersoever thou wentest</u>, and have <u>cut off all thine enemies out of thy sight</u>, and have <u>made thee a great name</u>, like unto the name of the great men that are in the earth.

10 Moreover I will appoint a place for my people Israel, and will plant them, that they may dwell in a place of their own, and move no more; neither shall the children of wickedness afflict them any more, as beforetime,

11 And as since the time that I commanded judges to be over my people Israel, and have caused thee to <u>rest from all thine enemies</u>. Also the LORD telleth thee that <u>he will make thee an house</u>.

12 And when <u>thy days be fulfilled</u>, and thou shalt sleep with thy fathers, I <u>will set up thy seed after thee</u>, which shall proceed out of thy bowels, and I <u>will establish his kingdom.</u>

13 He shall build an house for my name, and I will stablish the throne of his kingdom for ever.

14 I will be his father, and he shall be my son. If he commit iniquity, I will chasten him with the rod of men, and with the stripes of the children of men:

15 But <u>my mercy shall not depart away from him</u>, as I took it from Saul, whom I put away before thee.

16 <u>And thine house and thy kingdom shall be established for ever before thee</u>: thy throne shall be established for ever.

The requirements of God's covenant with David are similar to Abraham's. We see that in David's own instructions to Solomon when David appointed him as successor to the throne. 1 Kings 2:3-4 states, "v3 And keep the charge of the LORD thy God, to <u>walk in his ways</u>, to <u>keep his statutes</u>, and his commandments, and his judgments, and his testimonies, as it is written in the law of Moses, that thou mayest prosper in all that thou doest, and whithersoever thou turnest thyself: v4 That the LORD may continue his word which he spake concerning me, saying, If thy children take heed to their way, to <u>walk before me in truth with all their heart and with all their soul</u>, there shall not fail thee (said he) a man on the throne of Israel." Although David failed God in some big ways, nevertheless he was known as the man after God's own heart.

Abraham and David responded to God's covenant with them. Even though they did not see all the parts of the covenant fulfilled in their life time (because some parts referred to their far future), they did enjoy many blessings God had promised them in the covenant while they lived. Their response to God's covenant was made by faith. Abraham's faith was accounted as righteousness by God. We too have to respond to the covenant of God by faith.

The New Covenant of God

What then has God's covenant with David got to do with us? You see that everlasting kingdom, that everlasting throne points to Jesus Christ, our new covenant with God (Hebrews 1:5; 8:7-13).

Hebrews 8:7-13

7 For if that first covenant had been faultless, then should no place have been sought for the second.

8 For finding fault with them, he saith, Behold, the days come, saith the Lord, when I will make a new covenant with the house of Israel and with the house of Judah:

9 Not according to the covenant that I made with their fathers in the day when I took them by the hand to lead them out of the land of Egypt; because they continued not in my covenant, and I regarded them not, saith the Lord.

10 For this is the covenant that I will make with the house of Israel after those days, saith the Lord; I will put my laws into their mind, and write them in their hearts: and I will be to them a God, and they shall be to me a people:

11 And they shall not teach every man his neighbour, and every man his brother, saying, Know the Lord: for all shall know me, from the least to the greatest.

12 For I will be merciful to their unrighteousness, and their sins and their iniquities will I remember no more.

13 In that he saith, A new covenant, he hath made the first old. Now that which decayeth and waxeth old is ready to vanish away.

Abraham and David both had the old covenant but we have the new covenant. The two covenants are essentially the same. It is partially inaccurate to say that the new covenant is better than the old. God is the same God who established the old and new covenant, but the manifestation in the new covenant is better because instead of the old priesthood and sacrificial system, Jesus became our sacrifice once and for all and He also became our great High Priest who now lives on to interceded for us. Hebrews 7:22 states, "By so much was Jesus made a surety of a better testament."

John 3:16, "For God so loved the world that He gave His only begotten son …" God initiated salvation for us because He so loved us. He so loved us that He gave. What made His love even more amazing is this; Romans 5:8 states that God demonstrated His love toward us, in that while we were still sinners … and in verse 10 it says that when we were enemies …" While we were using His name as a swear word, while we were mocking and persecuting believers, while we were making fun of His Holy word and tearing the witness of Christians down, while we were doing things that were an abomination to Him_and exalting the devil with our words and actions … God demonstrated His love to us!!!

You see, even before we care to make any response to God—in fact we were His enemies, God so loved us and He demonstrated His love for us by giving His only begotten son to die on the cross for our sins so that "whoever believes in Him should not perish but have everlasting life." "Whoever believes" is the part of the human response. That is faith. Entering into the new covenant of God in Jesus Christ is the first step of becoming a citizen of heaven. If you are not already a believer, what is your response to God's covenant through Jesus Christ, today? The lack of response is still a response.

The covenant has been initiated by God but if there is no human response, the benefits of the covenant exists but the unbelieving person will not reap nor taste of its benefits. If Abraham and David did not make the appropriate response to God, they would not have received the promises God had for them. And even if you are already a believer but you have doubts about God and His promises, you will not be able to taste the fullness of your benefits and spiritual inheritance while here on earth. **A true citizen of heaven is in covenant with God through Jesus Christ.**

Chapter 2

A True Citizen of Heaven Knows the Covenant God

When you enter into the new covenant of God in Jesus Christ, the covenant God becomes your God. What does that mean? Who is this covenant God? The name "God" has become a general name for many religious or even secular description of the Supreme Being. But not every reference of God refers to this covenant God that is mentioned here. We must differentiate between the covenant God and the general use of the name God that has no specific reference to the covenant God. A true citizen of heaven has to know his God in order to have surety and confidence to trust Him all the way. He has to know his God in order to know his purpose in the kingdom of God. The Almighty God is your God. The Sovereign God is your God. The Creator and ruler of the Universe is your God. The King of kings and the Lord of lords is your God.

The Natural Qualities of our Covenant God
1. The Omnipotent God, the All-powerful God

He has power to help you overcome your weaknesses. He has power to help you walk in victory. He has power to help you deal with your debts. He has power to help you overcome your fears. He has power to help you defeat your enemies. He can do all things. He has power to make a way when there is no way. His word says, "If God be for us, who can be against you?" Psalm 62:11 (NKJV): "God has spoken once. Twice I have heard this: That power belongs to God." There is no limit to His power. Nothing is impossible for Him (Luke 1:37). However, He will not do anything that is contrary to His nature.

2. The Omniscient God, the All-knowing God

He knows your pain. He knows your troubles. He knows your needs. He knows your loneliness. He knows all things. He knows what you are going to say even before you pray. He knows your thoughts and what is in your heart. Nothing escapes His knowledge, neither is there anything outside His knowledge. In John 21:17, Peter said this to Jesus, "… Lord, thou knowest all things; …"

Isaiah 40:13 indicates that God needing no teaching; "Who hath directed the Spirit of the LORD, or being his counsellor hath taught him?" Romans 11:33-36 supports the same theme, "O the depth of the riches both of the wisdom and knowledge of God! how unsearchable are his judgments, and his ways past finding out! For who hath known the mind of the Lord? or who hath been his counsellor? Or who hath first given to him, and it shall be recompensed unto him again? For of him, and through him, and to him, are all things: to whom be glory for ever. Amen".

He is able to give you knowledge, understanding and wisdom for your studies, and for your work. Psalm 147:5 states, "Great is our Lord, and of great power: his understanding is infinite".

3. The Omnipresence God, the Ever Present God

Where ever you are, He is there with you. He sees and watches over you throughout the day and in the night because He is a God that neither slumbers nor sleeps (Psalm 121). He is present everywhere at the same time! And because God is everywhere at the same time and that He knows everything, that means He knows everything simultaneously. Psalm 139:7-8, "Whither shall I go from thy spirit? or whither shall I flee from thy presence? If I ascend up into heaven, thou art there: if I make my bed in hell, behold, thou art there". Jeremiah 23:24 states, "Can any hide himself in secret places that I shall not see him? saith the LORD. Do not I fill heaven and earth? saith the LORD."

4. The Eternal God

Although God does not live in time or limited by time, eternity is the relationship of God and time. "But, beloved, be not ignorant of this one thing, that one day is with the Lord as a thousand years, and a thousand years as one day" (2 Peter 3:8 - NKJV). We are the ones that live in time and are limited by time.

"The eternal God is thy refuge, and underneath are the everlasting arms: and he shall thrust out the enemy from before thee; and shall say, Destroy them" (Deuteronomy 33:27). God has always been God. He is still God. He will always be God. God has always been around. Our past, our present and our future are all known to Him. He is still here and will always be around. He is here for you today. He will be here for your children for their tomorrows. "The four living creatures, each having six wings, were full of eyes around and within. And they do not rest day or night, saying: " Holy, holy, holy, Lord God Almighty, Who was and is and is to come!" (Revelation 4:8 – NKJV)

5. The Immutable God, the God who does not Change

"Jesus Christ the same yesterday, and to day, and for ever." (Hebrews 13:8 – NKJV) Jesus is the expressed image of God (1:3). Chapter 1:12 also states, "And as a vesture shalt thou fold them up, and they shall be changed: but thou art the same, and thy years shall not fail". These mean that because God does not change. What He did in the past for us, He can do it again today and also for all our tomorrows. There is thus a certainty and steadfastness in our God. His character does not change. James 1:17 describes God as "... the Father of lights, with whom is no variableness, neither shadow of turning". His truth, His words, and His promises do not change. "For ever, O LORD, thy word is settled in heaven" (Psalm 119:89). He is reliable all throughout our lives.

The Moral Qualities of our Covenant God

1. God is Holy

The word holy comes from a root word meaning "to separate". It has a reference to God's moral perfection or excellence. He is separated from evil and that which is unclean. This quality of holiness is the standard for man's attitudes, motives and actions. Being holy, He expects His children to be holy. "Be ye holy; for I am holy" states 1 Peter 1:16. We were translated from the kingdom of darkness to His Kingdom. Therefore as citizens of God's Kingdom we must allow the Holy Spirit to bring transformation in our lives so that we walk in holiness.

2. God is Righteous

Righteousness has to do with conforming to a certain standard of making the paths straight. God acts on the basis of His holy nature and He always does what is right, just and fair. Since He does not change, His actions are consistently right. Whatever He does He does it for the ultimate good of His people. We may not always understand His ways and plans but we can be comforted to know He always have our good in mind.

3. God is Love

This depicts the self-giving nature of God. It is out of His love for us that He provided a way for us to be reconciled back to Him. He loves and He gave. While we were yet enemies Christ died for our sins. It is His love that He seeks what is good for us. Jeremiah 29:11 says that His thoughts for us are for good and not for evil, to give us a future and a hope. There is nothing that can separate us from His love. The only one that can decide to walk away from His love is our own choice. "[38]For I am persuaded, that neither death, nor life, nor angels, nor principalities, nor powers, nor things present, nor things to come, [39]Nor height, nor depth, nor any other creature, shall be able to separate us from the love of God, which is in Christ Jesus our Lord." (Romans 8:38-39)

4. God is Truth

There is no falseness in God, neither deception. He is distinct from false gods. God's truth is the foundation of all knowledge. When Jesus said that He is the Way, the Truth and the Life, He is embodying truth. He is steadfast in His faithfulness toward us. Since God is truthful in His dealings with us, He expects us to relate with others in truth too. When people do not relate to one another in truth many social problems will arise.

We must also relate with Him in truth. In John 4:24 we are told to worship God in Spirit and in truth. There must be sincerity and genuineness of the heart in our relationship with Him.

5. God is Good

The goodness of God includes His love, grace, mercy and kindness. We have discussed about His love in point 3. The grace of God is His unmerited favor toward us. We received from Him what we do not deserve. That favor was based on His goodness. The greatest expression of His grace toward us is His plan of salvation through the death of His own dear Son.

His mercy is manifested in His compassion, patience and long-suffering. We see it in His forgiveness. He knows our weakness and the inclination to sin and offers forgiveness if we confess our sin. Even when we break our covenant with Him, in His mercy He maintains the covenantal relationship with us and shows us steadfast love and faithfulness. He shows us kindness. When we are distressed, He shows us kindness and delivers us from our afflictions.

Some of the Names of our Covenant God

1. Jehovah-Jireh, the Lord will provide, is your God.

Abraham called on the name of God by this name when God provided a ram as a burnt offering instead of his son. "And Abraham lifted up his eyes, and looked, and behold behind him a ram caught in a thicket by his horns: and Abraham went and took the ram, and offered him up for a burnt offering in the stead of his son. And Abraham called the name of that place Jehovah-Jireh: as it is said to this day, In the mount of the LORD it shall be seen" (Genesis 22:13-14).

God is able to provide for our physical needs. Matthew 6:30-34 shows that God cares about what we wear and what we eat and drink. "Wherefore, if God so clothe the grass of the field, which to day is, and to morrow is cast into the oven, shall he not much more clothe you, O ye of little faith? Therefore take no thought, saying, What shall we eat? or, What shall we drink? or, Wherewithal shall we be clothed? (For after all these things do the Gentiles seek:) for your heavenly Father knoweth that ye have need of all these things. But seek ye first the kingdom of God, and his righteousness; and all these things shall be added unto you. Take therefore no thought for the morrow: for the morrow shall take thought for the things of itself. Sufficient unto the day is the evil thereof."

More than just material needs, God cares and provides also for our spiritual needs. 2 Corinthians 9:8-10 states, "And God is able to make all grace abound toward you; that ye, always having all sufficiency in all things, may abound to every good work: (As it is written, He hath dispersed abroad; he hath given to the poor: his righteousness remaineth for ever. Now he that ministereth seed to the sower both minister bread for your food, and multiply your seed sown, and increase the fruits of your righteousness;" In similar light, 2 Peter 1:3 states, "According as his divine power hath given unto us all things that pertain unto life and godliness, through the knowledge of him that hath called us to glory and virtue:"

The problem here is that we are most of the time more concerned about our physical welfare than our spiritual. Be honest and listen to our prayers and we know that is true. Again Matthew 6:30-34 tells us not to be overly worried. There is an emphasis of God's concern for our physical welfare.

30Wherefore, <u>if God so clothe the grass of the field, which to day is, and to morrow is cast into the oven, shall he not much more clothe you, O ye of little faith?</u>

33<u>But seek ye first the kingdom of God, and his righteousness; and all these things shall be added unto you.</u>

We forget that if we have all our physical needs met and if we lose our souls, it is eternal tragedy. Matthew 16:26 clearly states this grim fact. "For what is a man profited, if he shall gain the whole world, and lose his own soul? or what shall a man give in exchange for his soul?"

2. Jehovah-Rapha, the Lord that heals, is your God

We were introduced to this name of God at the time when the Israelites were complaining about not being able to find good clean drinking water in the wilderness. "And he cried unto the LORD; and the LORD shewed him a tree, which when he had cast into the waters, the waters were made sweet: there he made for them a statute and an ordinance, and there he proved them, And said, If thou wilt diligently hearken to the voice of the LORD thy God, and wilt do that which is right in his sight, and wilt give ear to his commandments, and keep all his statutes, I will put none of these diseases upon thee, which I have brought upon the Egyptians: for I am the LORD that healeth thee" (Exodus 15:25-26).

God who created us is able to heal our body. Job 10:11 indicates that He knows every part of our body because He fashioned it; "Thou hast clothed me with skin and flesh, and hast fenced me with bones and sinews". Adam and Eve were created with no health problems. When sin came in so did health problems. However, through Jesus Christ, God made the way for us to have healing. Isaiah 53:5 indicates what Jesus did for us; "But he was wounded for our transgressions, he was bruised for our iniquities: the chastisement of our peace was upon him; and with his stripes we are healed". It is God's intention for His people to be healthy. God not only want us to prosper in our bodies but also in our souls. "Beloved, I wish above all things that thou mayest prosper and be in health, even as thy soul prospereth" (3 John 2). He is also able to heal our broken hearts. Psalm 147:3 shows that, "He healeth the broken in heart, and bindeth up their wounds".

3. Jehovah-Shalom, the Lord is peace, is your God.

Judges 6 relates how God enlisted Gideon for war with a very small army of 300 men. The Midianites and the Amalekites that Gideon had to go against were "as numerous as locusts; and their camels were without number, as the sand by the seashore in multitude" (7:12). Against this backdrop the Lord spoke peace into Gideon and told him not to fear for he that he would not die. "Then Gideon built an altar there unto the LORD, and called it Jehovahshalom: unto this day it is yet in Ophrah of the Abiezrites" (Judges 6:24).

God can give you peace where there is fear and torment. 2 Timothy 1:7, "For God hath not given us the spirit of fear; but of power, and of love, and of a sound mind". God can speak peace into the storms of your life. Jesus "rebuked the wind, and said unto the sea, Peace, be still. And the wind ceased, and there was a great calm" (Mark 4:39).

4. El-Shaddai, the God that is more than enough, is your God.

From Genesis 17:1-2 we note that Abraham was faced with a problem that was beyond him. He and his wife were way beyond child-bearing years. "And when Abram was ninety years old and nine, the LORD appeared to Abram, and said unto him, I am the Almighty God (El-Shaddai); walk before me, and be thou perfect. And I will make my covenant between me and thee, and will multiply thee exceedingly". But God said that He is able to do far more exceedingly than Abraham could think of.

The picture of God's almightiness here is not one of flexing arms but that of a woman's breast giving life and nourishment to a crying child who otherwise would not rest and be comforted. God gives out of His abundance. Abraham was restless from his childlessness but God was revealing to him that God can make nations out of him. El-Shaddai is more than enough for you. He can bring abundance and fruitfulness out of barrenness. There are no problems too big for Him. There are no obstacles too big that He cannot remove.

5. Adonai Jehovah, the Lord or Master, is your God.

This name was first found in Genesis 15:1-2; "After these things the word of the LORD came unto Abram in a vision, saying, Fear not, Abram: I am thy shield, and thy exceeding great reward. And Abram said, LORD God (Adonai Jehovah), what wilt thou give me, seeing I go childless, and the steward of my house is this Eliezer of Damascus?"

The name Adonai means "lord" or "master". This word when applied to man shows two kinds of earthly relationships: a master and his servant; and that of a husband to his wife. This same name is applied to God showing that there is a relationship between God and man; as Master and servant; and as Husband and wife. In these relationships with man, God loves and cares for the man to the uttermost. He cares for you as a loving and kind master to a servant. Psalm 123:2 states, "Behold, as the eyes of servants look unto the hand of their masters, and as the eyes of a maiden unto the hand of her mistress; so our eyes wait upon the LORD our God, until that he have mercy upon us".

He cares for you as a devoted husband to the wife. Song of Solomon 7:10 gives that picture of devotion, "I am my beloved's, and his desire is toward me". Hosea 2:16, 19-20 states, "And it shall be at that day, saith the LORD, that thou shalt call me Ishi (my husband); and shalt call me no more Baali (my lord) ... And I will betroth thee unto me for ever; yea, I will betroth thee unto me in righteousness, and in judgment, and in lovingkindness, and in mercies. I will even betroth thee unto me in faithfulness: and thou shalt know the LORD".

The covenant God becomes your all in all. The covenant God is faithful and He keeps all His promises to you. 2 Corinthians 1:20: "For all the promises of God in Him are Yes, and in Him

Amen, ..." He will not break His covenant with you. When your marriage covenant has been broken and your heart is broken in two, the covenant God remains true and will not break His covenant with you. When your job or business contract is broken, the covenant God remains true and will not break His covenant with you. When your friends break their friendship with you, the covenant God remains true and will not break His covenant with you. When your own family turns you away, the covenant God remains true and will not break His covenant with you. When the church circle rejects you, the covenant God remains true and will not break His covenant with you. When legal and health systems fail you, the covenant God remains true and will not break His covenant with you. He can mend a broken heart. "A bruised reed He will not break ... (Matthew 12:20).

What He did for you yesterday, He can do it again today. He can do it again tomorrow. You may not be faithful in keeping your part of the covenant but He remains faithful. I remember this story told many years ago. Since it has been quite a while back, I must confess that it may not be as accurate as it was first told, but the gist of the story is this: There was an elderly couple in a car. The man has been driving down the same road with his wife as usual for years. By and by, the woman asked her husband why he was not sitting near her anymore. The man paused for a while and then replied, "Dear, I have been sitting in the same position driving all these years. You are the one that have moved!"

The covenant God is still in the same position. He has been with you on your journey through life right from the time you were born; through the times you did not know Him; through the times you did not acknowledge Him as your God; through the times that you want Him out of your life; through the times that you said you did it all by your own hands ... He traveled with you. Silently, patiently, lovingly He watched over you without you ever knowing. You may never know in this life time, how many times

He intervened in your life to save you; to prevent something worst from happening to you. He is the same yesterday, today and forever. God is in that same position towards you.

There are many other characteristics and names of God. The list given is to help you know your covenant God a little better. It is important that we increasingly know our covenant God. Our knowledge of God (not head knowledge but a knowing in the heart and deep in one's spirit) affects every area of our lives; from the way we pray to our zeal for Him; from our relationship with Him to our relationship with others. With knowledge of God, only then we can have the right perspective and concept of God and thus relate to Him as true citizen of heaven. A distorted or wrong image of God does not build our confidence, trust or faith in Him. When we do not have confidence in Him, we cannot function as true citizen of heaven. **A true citizen of heaven knows his God with whom he is in covenant with.**

Chapter 3

A True Citizen of Heaven, Must know and follow the terms in the Covenant

Every contract has terms of agreement. It is the same with our Covenant with God. For some reason many New Testament believers think that the Old Testament and its laws, which really is the "terms of agreement", do not apply to them anymore. Perhaps that is why there is so much lawlessness even in the church today. In the prologue the passage of 2 Timothy 3:2-6 was cited. We see these characteristics mentioned in that passage blatantly displayed in the church today.

The God of the Old Testament is still the same God of the New Testament. God has not changed. Malachi 3:6 states, "For I am the LORD, I change not …" If He is still the same God then why would we think that the terms of the Covenant in the Old Testament has changed in the New Testament? What He has put into place in the terms of the Covenant has not changed either.

The laws of the Old Testament have its continuity in the New Testament. Jesus was a Jew. The Apostles who carried on the work of Jesus were Jews. Paul who wrote most of the New Testament was also a Jew. They all learnt and practiced the laws that God had stipulated for them in the Covenant. They did not have the New Testament yet when they started to minister. They only had the Old Testament and it was from the Old Testament that they taught from.

Much of the exhortations and teachings found in the New Testament is an extension from the Ten Commandments.

Exodus 20:1-17

[1]And God spake all these words, saying,

[2]I am the LORD thy God, which have brought thee out of the land of Egypt, out of the house of bondage.

[3]Thou shalt have no other gods before me.

[4]Thou shalt not make unto thee any graven image, or any likeness of any thing that is in heaven above, or that is in the earth beneath, or that is in the water under the earth.

[5]Thou shalt not bow down thyself to them, nor serve them: for I the LORD thy God am a jealous God, visiting the iniquity of the fathers upon the children unto the third and fourth generation of them that hate me;

[6]And shewing mercy unto thousands of them that love me, and keep my commandments.

[7]Thou shalt not take the name of the LORD thy God in vain; for the LORD will not hold him guiltless that taketh his name in vain.

[8]Remember the sabbath day, to keep it holy.

[9]Six days shalt thou labour, and do all thy work:

[10]But the seventh day is the sabbath of the LORD thy God: in it thou shalt not do any work, thou, nor thy son, nor thy daughter, thy manservant, nor thy maidservant, nor thy cattle, nor thy stranger that is within thy gates:

[11]For in six days the LORD made heaven and earth, the sea, and all that in them is, and rested the seventh day: wherefore the LORD blessed the sabbath day, and hallowed it.

[12] Honour thy father and thy mother: that thy days may be long upon the land which the LORD thy God giveth thee.

[13] Thou shalt not kill.

[14] Thou shalt not commit adultery.

[15] Thou shalt not steal.

[16] Thou shalt not bear false witness against thy neighbour.

[17] Thou shalt not covet thy neighbour's house, thou shalt not covet thy neighbour's wife, nor his manservant, nor his maidservant, nor his ox, nor his ass, nor any thing that is thy neighbour's.

The first five items on the Ten Commandments shows us how to relate to our covenant God. The second five items shows us how to relate with others. It is significant that we were told how to relate and walk with God first. It puts things in the right perspective: God before others and self. Jesus gave this answer to a lawyer in Matthew 22:36-40.

[36] Master, which is the great commandment in the law?

[37] Jesus said unto him, Thou shalt love the Lord thy God with all thy heart, and with all thy soul, and with all thy mind.

[38] This is the first and great commandment.

[39] And the second is like unto it, Thou shalt love thy neighbour as thyself.

[40] On these two commandments hang all the law and the prophets.

In every contract it pays to follow through when we agree with the terms stipulated. If any part of the terms of the contract is broken there are consequences. It is much the same way. Deuteronomy 28 gives a vivid picture of the blessings of God when we obey the commandments He has set for us and the consequences if we disobeyed.

Deuteronomy 28:1-2

[1] "And it shall come to pass, if thou shalt hearken diligently unto the voice of the LORD thy God, to observe and to do all his commandments which I command thee this day, that the LORD thy God will set thee on high above all nations of the earth:

[2] And all these blessings shall come on thee, and overtake thee, if thou shalt hearken unto the voice of the LORD thy God."

Deuteronomy 28: 14-15

[14] "And thou shalt not go aside from any of the words which I command thee this day, to the right hand, or to the left, to go after other gods to serve them.

[15] But it shall come to pass, if thou wilt not hearken unto the voice of the LORD thy God, to observe to do all his commandments and his statutes which I command thee this day; that all these curses shall come upon thee, and overtake thee:"

When God set something for us to follow, we have to follow it to the last detail. We cannot mix it with other things, like for example, bringing in other forms of practice and beliefs from former pagan ways. When we entered a covenant with God, we were set apart for Him to do His way and His will. The terms in the covenant are God's values. If we are to rule and reign with Jesus Christ, the King of Kings, we need to know His kingly values. Many believers are excited to rule and reign with Christ but how do we rule and reign with Christ when we do not know what it takes to rule with Him? **So, a true citizen of heaven must know and follow the terms in the Covenant.**

Chapter 4

A True Citizen of Heaven, Is a Part of the Covenant People

We originally belonged to God and therefore to God's kingdom. The evidence is in scripture. God, the King of His kingdom, created and fashioned us in our mother's womb (Job 31:15; Psalms 139:13; Isaiah 49:5). [5] "Before I formed thee in the belly I knew thee; and before thou camest forth out of the womb I sanctified thee, and I ordained thee a prophet unto the nations." (Jeremiah 1:5) Before you were declared a citizen of your natural country at birth, you were a spiritual citizen of God's kingdom. But as soon as we were born, our spiritual citizenship was changed. We became citizens of another spiritual kingdom—the kingdom of darkness.

Citizens or permanent residents in the kingdom of darkness, according to Ephesians 6:12, are under rulers of darkness and wicked spiritual hosts. [12] "For we wrestle not against flesh and blood, but against principalities, against powers, against the rulers of the darkness of this world, against spiritual wickedness in high places." These rulers of darkness have only one intention—to destroy you. John 10:10 states, "The thief (devil) does not come except to steal, and to kill, and to destroy …"

In order for us to be delivered from being the citizens of

the kingdom of darkness and translated back to the kingdom of light, the covenant God made a way for us through Jesus Christ. Colossians 1:13 states that "He had delivered us from the power of darkness and conveyed (translated) us into the kingdom of the Son of His love." Earlier we established the fact that when we responded by faith to the new covenant through Jesus Christ, the covenant God has become our God. That also means we are now rightfully citizens of God's kingdom. Adam and Eve sold their citizenship rights to the devil. That had a domino effect on every human being born. But through faith in Jesus Christ, who has defeated the enemy, we can once again become citizens of the kingdom of God.

Jesus, the Head of Church

The people of the new covenant are citizens of the kingdom of God. In earthly terms, the people of the new covenant are what we know today as the church, the body of Christ. 1 Corinthians 12:27 states, "Now you are the body of Christ, and members individually." And Jesus is the head of the church which is His body (Ephesians 5:23). Here is the part we must always remember. As a covenant people, the church, who is the body of Christ; *we must live, move and have our being* in Jesus who is the head (Acts 17:28). Our new covenant with God had a jump start in Jesus Christ. This new covenant has to also continue in Jesus Christ until He comes to take us home to our heavenly Kingdom with God.

To illustrate this point I want to share a duck slaughtering event. Around the Chinese New Year festival, the Chinese in my country of origin would give each other gifts, such as, peanuts, oranges, sweet cakes, baskets of food and in years past, live chicken and ducks too! In other countries the Chinese would do things a little different. One particular Chinese New Year we were given a duck. My mother was afraid to slaughter it. I was just as scared. It is the sight of blood that makes me weak all over. My father was working. So my mother asked my brother to slaughter the duck. In those days, you do not have the luxury of buying them all cleaned and packed like the grocery stores today. He had no choice. He was the man! My brother is about four years younger than I. He was probably only eleven then.

So he held the duck down. We watched from afar. With one butcher knife chop, he severed the duck's head from the rest of the body. I know it is gruesome but he had no prior experience. To our horror the headless body of the duck got up and started waddling away wildly. We all screamed and ran in panic. My brother did not know what to do. It was unexpected. How could a duck without its head still move around? The duck, of course without the head, had no sense of direction. It waddled on from one direction to another until it finally lost all of its life.

The point of this event is for us to note that many times in the body of Christ, either individually or corporately, we carry on as a church without letting Jesus be the head, leading and guiding us by His holy spirit. With increased knowledge, skills, and technologies it is so easy to carry on church or life with our own plans, and our own programs. Is it the plan for the covenant people of God, to carry on without Jesus and His holy spirit? We have a form of religion but no life. Why? It is because we become headless people of the new covenant. The body is cut off from the head. A body cut off from the head will soon lose its life. That's why sometimes our life seems so dead and our services seem so dead. So, as a covenant people, the church, who is the body of Christ; we must start with Christ, continue in Christ—we must live, move and have our being in Jesus who is the head (Acts 17:28).

A Continual Response to the Covenant

Like Abraham and David who made not just a one time

response but a continual response to the covenant, we too must make that continual response. What then is the continuing purpose of the church in relation to the covenant of God? The covenant is continuous and so we must make that continuous response.

To illustrate, when a negotiation between two parties is successful and a contract is signed, both parties expect the terms to be continuously carried out. The signing of the contract is the first concrete response but the expectation is that after the signing of the contract, the terms in the contract continues and the parties involved continues to make the appropriate responses or else there will be a breach. It is similar to our response to God's covenant. I said similar because in man's contract when you breach it, you pay for it, every single cent. In God's covenant, when we break it; but if we repent from that breach, He shows mercy by giving us a brand new start and forgives us off all that is past. He is not going to be calculative of every single term we break. He forgives all that surrounds that breach of the covenant.

Let's look at the definition of a church to better understand why the covenant people need to make continuous response to the covenant of God. The Greek word for church is *ekklesia* meaning "called out" or "summoned" from their respective places to discuss something of interest to the community. A group of people (in this case us, the church) has been called out to assemble by an appropriate authority and that is, the covenant God. This people are therefore are a special group of people. The covenant people are a special group of people that God have called out.

A People Called out from Idolatry

First, what are the covenant people, the citizens of heaven, called out from? Abraham was called out by God from an idolatrous people. God asked him to leave his country and go to a promised land that he did not even know about. Why? Was that necessary? Ur was the largest and wealthiest cities at that time. God knew if Abraham was to stay on in the idolatrous nation, Abraham would not be able to progressively discover who his covenant God is and enjoy communion with the one true God. Likewise, we the covenant people are called out by God from the kingdom of darkness to discover progressively who our covenant God is. We may have head knowledge about who our covenant God is, but we do not have a fixed, deep, immovable revelation of who He truly is.

For example, I did not have that deep heart's understanding of our covenant God as Jehovah Jireh, the Lord our provider, until He supernaturally provided for all my three years of tuition fees in the first Bible college I went to. An Australian couple, whom I have never met wrote to the Dean of the college and told him that they would support me. How they learnt of my needs, I did not know.

I did not have a deep heart's understanding of our covenant God as Jehovah Rapha, the Lord our healer, until he healed me of stroke in 2001. I am not saying that we have to go through something bad to discover God. Some people are so pliable in the spirit that they discover God easily. But in my case God had to break through my wavering faith in those areas so that I could discover Him. When we have a heart's understanding not head knowledge then we will be able to enjoy communion with our covenant God. We cannot discover God progressively and enjoy communion with Him if we are still clinging onto the kingdom of darkness. In a later chapter entitled, "Feasting and Drinking at the Table of the Kingdom of God", I will explain a little more on this subject.

To be called out from idolatry also means that the covenant people are called into a consecrated life. We are set apart unto godliness and holiness. God says, "Be holy as I am holy". We are in the world but we are not of the world. We are of God.

The covenant people are the house of covenant. The house of covenant is essentially the temple of the Holy Spirit. We grieve the Holy Spirit with our sins, and our self-will. There will be a feeling that something inside of us is shrinking. The shrinking feeling is that grieving of the Holy Spirit. You see, when we are being filled with the Holy Spirit, we feel an expansion and an enlarging inside of us. We always hear the word enlarging in scripture. At times it refers to the enlarging of what He is doing inside of us. When that enlarging comes inside of you, you feel what David likes to say, "my soul is satisfied." But when you grieve the Holy Spirit, your soul feels the defilement and it feels a restlessness and dissatisfaction.

<u>A People Called out from Bondage</u>

The covenant people are also called out from bondage. In Exodus we see that the Israelites were called out of bondage in Egypt. They were liberated from slavery. Similarly, we the covenant people are liberated from the power of slavery in the kingdom of darkness. There is power in the name of Jesus to deliver us from all kinds of bondages and addictions (addictions are forms of slavery) of alcohol, of nicotine, of gambling, of pornography, of impulsive shopping, of drugs, endless makeover and much more. God has called us out of these bondages and addictions. God wants us liberated to fulfill a glorious destiny. Rahab responded to the covenant God. She was called out of the bondage of prostitution to help Israel possess the Promised Land. In fact if you look at the genealogy of Jesus Christ in the first chapter of Matthew, Rahab was listed as an ancestor of Jesus

Christ. A glorious destiny indeed! But unfortunately many amongst the covenant people do not want to be set free because some of these bondages are pleasurable. And for that matter, they will not walk into their glorious destiny of the Lord.

Called out to be God's Special People

Second, what is the covenant people, the citizens of heaven called out to be? The covenant people are called out to be God's special people. By God's grace, God had chosen Abraham and his descendants to be His people. Isaiah 41:8-9 state, "... whom I have chosen. The descendants of Abraham My friend. You whom I have taken from the ends of the earth, and called from its farthest regions, And said to you, You are My servant, I have chosen you and have not cast you away;" The covenant people are Abraham's descendants. Galatians 3:29: "And if you are Christ's; then you are Abraham's seed, and heirs according to the promises."

I know of many believers who having made the response to the covenant of God by accepting Jesus; after a while have the attitude of "whatever", taking light the purposes of God's covenant. If we could grasp what 1 Peter 2:9-10 says, we will not have the attitude of "whatever". "But you are a chosen generation, a royal priesthood, a holy nation, His own special people, that you may proclaim the praises of Him who called you out of darkness into His marvelous light, who once were not a people but are now the people of God, who had not obtained mercy but now have obtained mercy". We no longer remain as just ordinary people; we are called to be God's royal priesthood, a holy nation, and God's own special people in His kingdom. What an honor. What favor, mercy and blessing you are going to receive. We are also called the children of God (John 1:13-14). In Jesus we have a marvelous inheritance.

A People Called out to Proclaim God's Praises

1) The Light and Salt

Third, what are the covenant people, the citizens of heaven, called out for? Our privileges as God's special people come with sobering responsibilities. We just read that the covenant people to "proclaim the praises of Him who called you out of darkness into His marvelous light," How do we proclaim the praises of God? Matthew 5:16 states, "Let your light so shine before men, that they may see your good works and glorify your Father in heaven." We can witness, talk all we want but if our lives are not in congruent with our words and the principles of God's word, our words do not hold water. In fact the name of Christ has been brought down not glorified many a times because our lives contradict the principles of God's word.

The lives of the covenant people are to be like salt and light so that people can see the testimony of our lives and glorify God. Salt has a preservative element. We helped preserved the society from getting worst. As true citizens of heaven we are to preserve righteousness and truth in our society not add on corruption and evil. Our testimonies should be like light that draws people to God. Matthew 5:13-15 states,

'13Ye are the salt of the earth: but if the salt have lost his savour, wherewith shall it be salted? it is thenceforth good for nothing, but to be cast out, and to be trodden under foot of men.

14Ye are the light of the world. A city that is set on an hill cannot be hid.

15Neither do men light a candle, and put it under a bushel, but on a candlestick; and it giveth light unto all that are in the house."

2) Unity

The covenant people also proclaim the praises of God through unity. John 17:21states, "that they may be one, as You, Father, are in Me, and I in You, that they also may be one in Us, that the world may believe that You sent Me". Although our relationship with God is very personal, it was never intended for the covenant people to live or serve in isolation, be it as an individual or group segregation or denomination or organization. In the chapter entitled, "A True Citizen of Heaven is in Covenant with The Body of Christ", gives a further explanation about why a true citizen is not an island. You cannot mature fully in isolation. You cannot fully influence any one for Christ in isolation. Most of all you cannot glorify God fully in isolation. I find this problem more and more in the city. We become very individualistic. God intended the covenant people to be a community of believers just like in the book of Acts. But individualists gather together as a community only when it is convenient and beneficial for them.

The people of the new covenant are "called out" by God for His glory and His purposes. A true citizen of heaven is part of the church, the body of Christ and Jesus is the head of the body. Having made the first concrete response to the our covenant God by accepting Jesus as our savior and Lord, a true citizen of heaven need to continue responding to the covenant made with God in Jesus. In Jesus we live and move and have our being. Our continual response is in the definition of a church. We are called out from idolatry to a consecrated and holy life. We are called to progressively discover our covenant God and enjoy our communion with Him. We are called out from bondage and addiction; liberated to walk into a glorious destiny. We are called out to be a special people of God, a royal priesthood, a holy nation, children of God, joint-heirs with Jesus Christ. We are called to proclaim the praises of God by being a light and being united with love (John 13:35: "By this all will know that you are My disciples, if you have love for one another). We are "called out" by God not just as an individual but as a group of people. **A true citizen of heaven is a part of the Covenant people.**

Chapter 5

A True Citizen of Heaven is in Covenant with the Body of Christ

A true citizen of heaven is not an island. God never intended for a believer to live in isolation. I John 1:7 states that "if we walk in the light, as he (God) is in the light, we have fellowship one with another". A believer is part of the body of Christ. 1 Corinthians 12:14, 18-27 describe the importance of each member to the whole body of Christ. The vitality of the life of a believer in Christ Jesus very much depends on the believer being connected with other believers.

The Body of Christ is Made up of Many Members

14For the body is <u>not one member, but many</u>.

18But now hath God set the members every one of them in the body, as it hath pleased him.

19And if they were all one member, where were the body?

20But now are they many members, yet but one body.

21And the eye cannot say unto the hand, I have no need of thee: nor again the head to the feet, I have no need of you.

22Nay, much more those members of the body, which seem to be more feeble, are necessary:

23And those members of the body, which we think to be less honourable, upon these we bestow more abundant honour; and our uncomely parts have more abundant comeliness.

24For our comely parts have no need: but God hath tempered the body together, having given more abundant honour to that part which lacked.

25That there should be no schism in the body; but that the members should have the same care one for another.

26And whether one member suffer, all the members suffer with it; or one member be honoured, all the members rejoice with it.

27Now ye are the body of Christ, and members in particular.

In the Kingdom of God, citizens not only have privileges but responsibilities and accountability to one another. These responsibilities are to flow from love for one another. If we love one another then God's love has been perfected in us.

1 John 4:7-12

7Beloved, let us love one another: for love is of God; and every one that loveth is born of God, and knoweth God.

8He that loveth not knoweth not God; for God is love.

9In this was manifested the love of God toward us, because that God sent his only begotten Son into the world, that we might live through him.

10Herein is love, not that we loved God, but that he loved us, and sent his Son to be the propitiation for our sins.

11Beloved, if God so loved us, we ought also to love one another.

12No man hath seen God at any time. If we love one another, God dwelleth in us, and his love is perfected in us.

A Relationship that Flows in Love

Love for one another is expressed in many ways. Romans 12:10 describes love as "Be kindly affectioned one to another with brotherly love; in honour preferring one another". Ephesians 4:2-3 states, "With all lowliness and meekness, with longsuffering, forbearing one another in love; Endeavouring to keep the unity of the Spirit in the bond of peace". In Hebrews 10:24 love is seen as provoking one another to love and to good works. 1 Peter 1:22 gives a call to have unfeigned or sincere love for the brethren and a love that is fervent from a pure heart. Love is to be "of one mind, having compassion one of another, love as brethren, be pitiful, be courteous: Not rendering evil for evil, or railing for railing: but contrariwise blessing; knowing that ye are thereunto called, that ye should inherit a blessing" (1 Peter 3:8-9).

    Each believer has a function or functions in the body of Christ. Romans 14:18-20 and 1 Thessalonians 5:10-12 both talk about edifying one another. We are to follow things that make for peace to one another. We are to comfort one another. Ephesians 4:7-16 and I Corinthians 12 give a whole list of the different functions of the members of the body of Christ. Ephesians 4:16 states, "From whom <u>the whole body fitly joined together</u> and compacted by that which every joint <u>supplieth</u>, according to the effectual working in the measure of every part, <u>maketh increase of the body unto the edifying of itself in love</u>".

<u>A Relationship Vital in Spiritual Warfare</u>
    Another vital element in the relationship of a believer to other believers is in the realm of spiritual warfare and upholding one another in prayer. There are times when a believer goes through tough times and cannot find the strength to prevail in prayer. We think of the Moses in Exodus 17:9-13 who needed Aaron and Hur to hold up his hand and also needed Joshua to lead the army of Israel into battle.

9And Moses said unto Joshua, Choose us out men, and go out, fight with Amalek: to morrow I will stand on the top of the hill with the rod of God in mine hand.

10So Joshua did as Moses had said to him, and fought with Amalek: and Moses, Aaron, and Hur went up to the top of the hill.

11And it came to pass, when Moses held up his hand, that Israel prevailed: and when he let down his hand, Amalek prevailed.

12But Moses hands were heavy; and they took a stone, and put it under him, and he sat thereon; and Aaron and Hur stayed up his hands, the one on the one side, and the other on the other side; and his hands were steady until the going down of the sun.

13And Joshua discomfited Amalek and his people with the edge of the sword.

Deuteronomy 32: 30 indicates the strength of corporate united prayer of believers in the Lord. "How should one chase a thousand, and two put ten thousand to flight, except their Rock had sold them, and the LORD had shut them up?"

In one of our prayer meetings I had an open vision about cogs in a lady's body. Every one of the cogs seems to be rotating except one. The one that was not working affected the speed and smooth rotation of the other cogs. While God revealed to her what that one cog represented, I, on the other hand saw a simile between the cogs' rotation and the function of each member to the whole body of Christ. If one member is not doing its part it does affect the other members of the body.

The Cause-Effects of Relationship Problems

There are many cause and effect problems concerning members of the body of Christ. In my observation the problem that is common and damaging that squeeze out love for one another has to do with careless conversations, gossips and slander. I Corinthians 3:3 states, "For ye are yet carnal: for whereas there is among you envying, and strife, and divisions, are ye not carnal, and walk as men?" Some do it out of sheer malice to undercut someone to obtain what the other has. Some do it out of jealousy to tear a person's reputation. Some do it out of poor self-image to exalt themselves and to bring the other down. Some just have a disease of the mouth that seems to enjoy digging up dirty laundry of others. Proverbs 6:19 shows the utter contempt of God towards those who bring division.

Proverbs 6:16-19

16These six things doth the <u>LORD hate: yea, seven are an abomination unto him</u>:

17A proud look, a lying tongue, and hands that shed innocent blood,

18An heart that deviseth wicked imaginations, feet that be swift in running to mischief,

19A false witness that speaketh lies, and <u>he that soweth discord among brethren</u>.

James 3:14-16

14But if ye have <u>bitter envying</u> and <u>strife</u> in your hearts, glory not, and <u>lie not against the truth</u>.

15This <u>wisdom descendeth not from above</u>, but is <u>earthly, sensual, devilish</u>.

16For where <u>envying and strife</u> is, there is <u>confusion and every evil work</u>.

    Instead of all that work of evil, true citizens of heaven, should cover sins of others with their love. The word used for love in the King James Version is charity. 1 Peter 4:8 states, "And above all things have fervent charity (love) among yourselves: for charity (love) shall cover the multitude of sins". If we would let love cover a multitude of sins then evil will not spread.

This reminds me of an allegory my youngest son thought of while we were weeding the backyard. He was six then. I had told him to pull the weeds by the roots in order to stop that particular weed from sprouting again. Enlightened, he commented to this effect; "That is like sin. Sin must be pulled up at the roots. If we just pull the plant up without the root, it will grow again. It will not only grow again but it will spread. The flower has seeds. When the wind blows on the flower, the seeds will be blown all over. The seeds will germinate and more weeds will grow. Sin must be pulled up at its roots or else it will spread; from one person to another, then to another and then the whole world!" I shuddered when he said the "whole world". That is something we do not want to happen to the church; the defilement of the whole body of Christ.

To walk in love and promote health in the body of Christ, true citizens of heaven should meditate on these recorded in Philippians 4:8, "Finally, brethren, whatsoever things are true, whatsoever things are honest, whatsoever things are just, whatsoever things are pure, whatsoever things are lovely, whatsoever things are of good report; if there be any virtue, and if there be any praise, think on these things". When we would think on those things; when we would esteem another better than ourselves; when we would choose to forgive and not hold on to an offense; then we are truly in covenant with one another.

Jesus is the expression of God's love. As citizens of heaven we too are to be the expression of God's love. A child usually has some physical resemblance of his or her father, as well as, certain traits of his of her father. Jesus was the expressed image of His father, according to Hebrews 1:3. So, as sons of God, we are to reflect more and more of Him. God is love and it should be only natural that we be the expression of God's love more and more. We cannot excuse ourselves saying that we cannot love a particular person or have no love at all because Romans 5:5 states that "the love of God is shed abroad in our hearts by the Holy Ghost which is given unto us". **A true citizen of heaven is in covenant with the body of Christ**

PART 2 KINGDOM OF GOD

Chapter 6

A True Citizen of Heaven, Intentionally Lives Under the Kingdom of God

The theme on the Kingdom of God permeates practically every subject in His Word. It covers our expressed behavior, our hidden motives, our purposes, our plans, and our relationships. The list is inexhaustible. As a true citizen of heaven we need to know the characteristics not only of the Kingdom of God but the kingdom of darkness so that we can intentionally make appropriate changes.

I want to bring some comparison of the characteristics of the kingdom of darkness that sprang forth when Adam and Eve fell and the characteristics of the Kingdom of God described in the beginning in Genesis 1. From this comparison, my prayer is that we will have a fuller understanding of how we are to intentionally live under the kingdom of God, not under the kingdom of darkness. We are in the world but we are not of the world. In John 17:16 Jesus said, "They are not of the world, even as I am not of the world." Because we are not of the world, we are to intentionally live as citizens of the Kingdom of God and not the kingdom of darkness.

In a previous chapter we were reminded that we were delivered from the power of the spiritual kingdom of darkness and translated back to the spiritual Kingdom of God (Colossians

1:13). That means we are no longer citizens under the rule of the rulers of darkness and wicked spiritual hosts but we are citizens under the rule of God in the spiritual Kingdom of God.

What was God's intention for citizens of His spiritual Kingdom? Let's look into the very beginning of Genesis 1:26-28.

26 "And God said, Let us make man in our image, after our likeness: and let them have dominion over the fish of the sea, and over the fowl of the air, and over the cattle, and over all the earth, and over every creeping thing that creepeth upon the earth.

27So God created man in his own image, in the image of God created he him; male and female created he them.

28And God blessed them, and God said unto them, Be fruitful, and multiply, and replenish the earth, and subdue it: and have dominion over the fish of the sea, and over the fowl of the air, and over every living thing that moveth upon the earth".

From this passage, we note that we were given dominion. That means we have absolute ownership. This is man's original position. Note that it is not dominion over man or each other. A controlling spirit over man or each other is never of God. Yes, God does put people in authority. However authority in God's Kingdom is like that of a shepherd to the sheep. The one in authority guides the sheep with his staff not use the staff to beat them up for control. A true shepherd-kind of authority leads the sheep to green pastures and still waters. Dominion over man is the characteristic of the kingdom of darkness. It is enslaving. Satan enslaves people to put them into bondage so that he can eventually destroy them.

You see, when God gives something, be it a material thing, a position or a ministry, to you, nothing or no one can take it away

53

from you. It belongs to you. You do not have to control people or circumstances to get something or keep something. When God gives to you, nothing and no one can take it away from you. Only God Himself can take it away from you or allow it to be taken away from you. So, have a reverent fear of God.

Our original position is a place of victory not defeat. We have absolute ownership over the animal world and territories (This is in the context of the spiritual realm.) Our original position is that we are above and not beneath. We are above the circumstances of our economy not under the circumstances. We are the head and not the tail. We are the blessed not the cursed. We increase and not diminish. We are the free not the bound.

The purposes and benefits for man go hand in hand. God blessed man to be fruitful and multiply; to replenish (to become full : fill up again - Webster) the earth and subdue (to conquer and bring into subjection - Webster). These are not terms of aimless living nor terms of lack neither is it bondage. These are terms that show us that God has blessed man with the power to increase and to possess.

It is so important that we know what God's intention is for us now that we are translated back into the Kingdom of the Son of His love. If we do not understand His original intention then we do not know our rights. We do not know our freedom. We do not know our benefits. We do not know our rich heavenly inheritance. We do not know our position. We do not know our purpose. We do not know the damage the enemy has already done. If we do not have an understanding of what the enemy has done then we will continue to live with the mentality subjected to the kingdom of darkness even though we have been translated to God's Kingdom.

To illustrate this: I am reminded of a parakeet my family once had. It was kept in a roomy cage. We took care of it as best as we knew how: fed it, gave it drink and cleaned the cage daily. We talked to it; we coaxed it to mimic us, whistled to it, and sang to it and it responded most of the time. After many months we decided to let it out of the cage. We put it out on the floor. We had the windows wide open and it had every chance to fly to freedom. But instead, to our surprise, it did not. In fact, it hopped over to a large tall mirror placed on the floor that we had in the living room. Looking at itself, it would sway from side to side and did an up- and-down motion with the feather on its neck all sticking up. Quite a vain parakeet it was. Normally it made high pitch sounds but when looking at the mirror it made a lower-tone sound. It was hilarious watching it. After a few days we figured what it was doing in front of the mirror. It thought there was another bird in front. It must have been doing a love dance of some sort. When it was satisfied, it would go back to the cage. Day after day it did that. It eventually died of old age.

The allegory here is this: the parakeet was caged (in the kingdom of darkness). After a few months it was set free to be a bird that it was originally intended to be (the kingdom of God). Although set free, the bird still had the mentality of being in a caged atmosphere. If we do not renew our minds as Paul tells us in Romans 12:2 ["And be not conformed to this world: but be ye transformed by the renewing of your mind, that ye may prove what is that good, and acceptable, and perfect, will of God"] we too will continue to live with the mindset of the kingdom of darkness. Why? We have lived in it as citizens too long. We become accustomed to its systems. We adapted to the conditions. So, even when we have been translated to the Kingdom of God, we still operate in the system of the kingdom of darkness. A paradigm shift occurs only as we know, believe and act on what God says about us in His word.

The parakeet actually was so accustomed to its cage that it kept going back in. It did not realize it was free to fly away. It was happy to be domesticated. In fact, it found a wonderful attraction that it keeps going back to, oblivious to the fact that that attraction was its own reflections. There are many things in the world offered by the kingdom of darkness that seem so alluring and so fun and we keep going back there. These are sources of distractions that keep us from the blessings God intended for us now that we are in His Kingdom. Like the parakeet fooled by its own reflections, these are deceptions of the enemy. Many of us are so bound by the devil and we do not even realize it.

The parakeet died as a "caged" bird when it could enjoy its freedom and have real mate not a reflection of itself in the mirror, if it had flown away. How sad. It is even sadder when we, the covenant people of God die in defeat and bondage, never fully knowing and reaping the benefits of God's kingdom.

The kingdom of darkness is bad news but the Kingdom of God is the good news. Here are some comparisons between the two kingdoms.

Genesis 3:14-19

14 "And the LORD God said unto the serpent, Because thou hast done this, thou art <u>cursed</u> above all cattle, and above every beast of the field; upon thy belly shalt thou go, and dust shalt thou eat all the days of thy life:

15And I will put <u>enmity</u> between thee and the woman, and between thy seed and her seed; it shall bruise thy head, and thou shalt bruise his heel.

16Unto the woman he said, I will greatly multiply thy <u>sorrow</u> and thy conception; in sorrow thou shalt bring forth children; and thy desire shall be to thy husband, and he shall rule over thee.

17And unto Adam he said, Because thou hast hearkened unto the voice of thy wife, and hast eaten of the tree, of which I commanded thee, saying, Thou shalt not eat of it: <u>cursed</u> is the ground for thy sake; in <u>sorrow</u> shalt thou eat of it all the days of thy life;

18Thorns also and thistles shall it bring forth to thee; and thou shalt eat the herb of the field;

19<u>In the sweat of thy face</u> shalt thou eat bread, till thou return unto the ground; for out of it wast thou taken: for dust thou art, and unto dust shalt thou return."

    Chapter 3 shows the consequences of Adam giving up his citizenship in God's Kingdom to the devil. These consequences show us the basic characteristics of the kingdom of darkness. Before then we only see the word, "blessed" but now we see the word, "cursed". Blessings belong to the Kingdom of God. Curses belong to the kingdom of darkness. What kind of curses are you facing? I recently heard a testimony of a lady that came to know the Lord. Everyone in her family died one by one and she, by the grace of God, is the only one alive today because she cried out to the God (not knowing at that time who He was). There was a curse in her family line but she cried out to God and was saved. Jesus has redeemed us from the curse of the law. If there is a recurring problem throughout the family line, it is most likely there is a curse somewhere.

    Before chapter 3 we picture unity and harmony in the creation of the world but now we see the word, "enmity". Love, unity and harmony belong to the Kingdom of God. I John 4:7 states that everyone who loves is born of God. Enmity belongs to the kingdom of darkness. Enmity is the friend of hate, segregations, racialism, discrimination, prejudice, violence, and anything that brings divisions amongst people. We should be at enmity with the devil (bruising him) but the devil has got us

57

making enemies of each other. Why? It is a clever tactic and strategy. We are sucked into it because of our foolish pride and fear of losing preeminence. If he has got us fighting each other then we cannot unite and focus our attack against him! He just folds his hands and laughs at us fighting each other. We make his job easier. Wake up, citizens of heaven! Awake, church! Your enemy is not people. It is the devil and all his cohorts.

Before the fall of man we have the picture of everything as good. Throughout chapter 1 we see the word "good". Good gives the feeling of joy and gladness. But in chapter 3 we see the word "sorrow". Good describes the Kingdom of God. Romans14:17 states, "For the Kingdom of God ... righteousness, and peace, and joy in the Holy Ghost". James 1:17 states that every good and perfect gift comes from God. Sorrow describes the kingdom of darkness. There is a sorrow that is godly but not in this context. The sorrow and pain of the kingdom of darkness comes from all forms of bondages and torments of body, soul and spirit. The devil assigns different spirits to torment us, to keep us in bondage, to keep us defeated. Are you tormented? It could be a spirit of physical abuse. It could be a spirit of infirmity. It could be a spirit of fear. It could be an immoral spirit. I heard a testimony of a girl who came out from a life-style of wild partying – orgies and all. One day God opened her eyes to see the spirit realm that shook her out of that lifestyle, a lifestyle she thought was nothing wrong if she did all the right things. She saw demons at every table and the dance floor, mingling with the crowd, carousing people and laughing away.

Before chapter 3, Adam and Eve had an easy life in the sense that it was not hard labor and toiling. God put everything they needed for them to enjoy. Have you ever wondered why God made man last? I see His great love for us when I considered it. He made everything else first so that Adam and Eve could enjoy His creation. Easy life, fulfillment, and satisfaction describe the

Kingdom of God. There is a work that we enjoy. Work was something God gave Adam. It brought purpose and meaning to his life. Adam was given a task over the animals and it was not stressful. Toil and hard laboring describes the kingdom of darkness. Does not our present life feel like it is hard laboring? Jesus said in Matthew 11:28-30; "28Come unto me, all ye that labour and are heavy laden, and I will give you rest. 29Take my yoke upon you, and learn of me; for I am meek and lowly in heart: and ye shall find rest unto your souls. 30For my yoke is easy, and my burden is light".

The good news of the Kingdom of God is in Jesus Christ.

Luke 4:18-19

18The Spirit of the Lord is upon me, because he hath anointed me to preach the gospel to the poor; he hath sent me to heal the brokenhearted, to preach deliverance to the captives, and recovering of sight to the blind, to set at liberty them that are bruised,

19To preach the acceptable year of the Lord".

Our position as citizens in the Kingdom of God is a place of victory, not defeat. We are above and not beneath. We are above the circumstances of our economy, not under the circumstances. We are the head and not the tail. We are the blessed not the cursed. We increase and not diminish. We are the free, not the bound. **A true citizen of heaven intentionally lives under the Kingdom of God.**

Chapter 7

A True Citizen of Heaven, Feasts and Drinks at the Table of the Kingdom of God

Whose table are you frequently feasting on? Is it the table of the kingdom of darkness or is it the table of the Kingdom of God? I Corinthians 10:16-22 distinguish clearly between drinking the cup of the Lord and drinking the cup of devils.

16The cup of blessing which we bless, is it not the communion of the blood of Christ? The bread which we break, is it not the communion of the body of Christ?

17For we being many are one bread, and one body: for we are all partakers of that one bread.

18Behold Israel after the flesh: are not they which eat of the sacrifices partakers of the altar?

19What say I then? that the idol is any thing, or that which is offered in sacrifice to idols is any thing?

20But I say, that the things which the Gentiles sacrifice, they sacrifice to devils, and not to God: and I would not that ye should have fellowship with devils.

21Ye cannot drink the cup of the Lord, and the cup of devils: ye cannot be partakers of the Lord's table, and of the table of devils.

22Do we provoke the Lord to jealousy? are we stronger than he?"

Although this passage talks about actual physical partaking of the cup or food, it does have a spiritual connotation - ye cannot be partakers of the Lord's table, and of the table of devils. We cannot feast and drink at the table of the kingdom of darkness and also feast and drink at the table of the Kingdom of God, and think that it is nothing and that there are no adverse effects.

Where we frequently feast and drink will determine what characteristics we will acquire. The common phrase is "What we eat is what we are". If we feast frequently at the table of the kingdom of darkness then we will eventually acquire the characteristics of the dark kingdom. It determines what kind of fruit are going to be produce in our lives. A bad tree cannot produce good fruits. Luke 6:43-46 depicts this;

43For a good tree bringeth not forth corrupt fruit; neither doth a corrupt tree bring forth good fruit.
44For every tree is known by his own fruit. For of thorns men do not gather figs, nor of a bramble bush gather they grapes.
45A good man out of the good treasure of his heart bringeth forth that which is good; and an evil man out of the evil treasure of his heart bringeth forth that which is evil: for of the abundance of the heart his mouth speaketh.
46And why call ye me, Lord, Lord, and do not the things which I say?"

Foul water cannot give good water. When we feast and drink from the kingdom of darkness we will become more and more like the devil.

Galatians 5:19-21 give a few examples of the fruit of the kingdom of darkness.
19Now the works of the flesh are manifest, which are these; Adultery, fornication, uncleanness, lasciviousness,

20Idolatry, witchcraft, hatred, variance, emulations, wrath, strife, seditions, heresies,

21Envyings, murders, drunkenness, revellings, and such like: of the which I tell you before, as I have also told you in time past, that they which do such things shall not inherit the kingdom of God.

Note the last verse. It says that those who do such things listed above "shall not inherit the Kingdom of God". One precious lady in our church has a powerful testimony about forgiveness. She said she died of diabetes and went to heaven. When she got to heaven there was a banquet and there were people who rejoicing and praising God. She found that she could not enter into the banquet. It was as if she was out of place. There were a few others like her. Then God asked her, "Would you like to enter in?" She replied, "Yes". God asked that question three times and three times she gave an affirmative answer. Then God said, "Go back to earth and forgive your in-laws". Her life was given back to her. She repented and forgave all her in-laws for every wrong they had done to her. That incident changed her completely. This testimony goes to show how serious God is about us bearing the fruit of the Kingdom of God and not bearing the fruit of the kingdom of darkness.

So what is this feasting and drinking at the table of the kingdom of darkness? If you are involved in palm reading, fortune telling, horoscope, and anything of the occult (being a game, a movie or not), you are feasting and drinking from the table of the kingdom of darkness. If you are watching pornography and any obscenity, you are feasting and drinking from the table of the kingdom of darkness. If you are reading anything that is not tested by the Spirit of God (no matter how harmless it looks), you are most likely feasting and drinking from the table of the kingdom of darkness. If you are seeking counsel not tested by the Spirit of

God (no matter how rational it feels), you are most likely also feasting and drinking from the table of the kingdom of darkness. If you are reading things and seeing things from any kind of media that is not tested by the Spirit of God, and you will find yourself talking more about the dark kingdom whereby magnifying the devil instead of magnifying God and His kingdom of light and love, then it is most likely you are feasting and drinking from the table of the kingdom of darkness. Yes, the bible talks about the devil and his works but the main theme throughout the bible is the glory of God, His salvation plan in His Son and His wonderful works and power, triumphing over the devil and his works.

The things you hear from conversations, the counsel you received, the things you see, the things you read, the things you are taught; have you allowed all these to be tested by the spirit of God? The Spirit of God is truth. In Him there is no deceit, no deception nor lies. The Spirit of God is holy. In Him there is neither evil nor wickedness. Everything must be tested by the Spirit of God. If not, the enemy can easily lead us into deception and evil by his subtle moves. If you wonder why conversations and counsels have led to dissensions and offences; it is because you have not allowed them to be tested by the Spirit of God and the enemy has found his way in. If you wonder why things you read and are taught have led to unbelief; it is because you have not allowed them to be tested by the Spirit of God and the enemy has found his way in. If you wonder why the things you see have led to lusts and ungodly desires, it is because you have not allowed them to be tested by the Spirit of God and the enemy has found his way in. All things must be tested by the Spirit of God. But if we keep feasting and drinking from the kingdom of darkness after we have been translated from the kingdom of darkness to the Kingdom of God's dear Son of love, we will never fully know how to test all things by the Spirit of God because we have allowed strange spirits of the kingdom of darkness to continue to lead us. I John 4:1 states, "Beloved, believe not every spirit, but try the spirits whether they are of God: …"

Jeremiah 2:13 gives a grave observation of the Lord concerning His people; "For my people have committed two evils; they have forsaken me the fountain of living waters, and hewed them out cisterns, broken cisterns, that can hold no water". After we have been saved by accepting Jesus Christ as our savior and Lord but when we keep going back to feast and drink from the kingdom of darkness, we are actually forsaking God who is the fountain of living waters. To feast and drink from cisterns that hold no water is feasting and drinking from the kingdom of darkness. Hold no water essentially describes that you are still famished. You are returning to evil, to carnality, to sensuality and coming out hungrier and thirstier in your souls than ever; angrier and dissatisfied than ever. This is the testing ground of whether we want to be a true citizen of Kingdom of God or the kingdom of the devil. 1 Kings 18:21 states, "And Elijah came unto all the people, and said, How long halt ye between two opinions? if the LORD be God, follow him: but if Baal, then follow him. And the people answered him not a word". There is another stark comparison in I Corinthians 6:16-20.

16"What? know ye not that he which is joined to an harlot is one body? for two, saith he, shall be one flesh.

17But he that is joined unto the Lord is one spirit.

18Flee fornication. Every sin that a man doeth is without the body; but he that committeth fornication sinneth against his own body.

19What? know ye not that your body is the temple of the Holy Ghost which is in you, which ye have of God, and ye are not your own?

20For ye are bought with a price: therefore glorify God in your body, and in your spirit, which are God's".

When we were translated to the Kingdom of God, we were joined to the Lord. Our body became the dwelling place of the Holy Spirit. We were bought with the precious blood of Jesus Christ. So, what business have we to be joined again to the "harlot", (figuratively referring to the devil), feasting and drinking from his table of darkness? II Corinthians 6:14-18 reiterates,

14 "Be ye not unequally yoked together with unbelievers: for what fellowship hath righteousness with unrighteousness? and what communion hath light with darkness?

15And what concord hath Christ with Belial? or what part hath he that believeth with an infidel?

16And what agreement hath the temple of God with idols? for ye are the temple of the living God; as God hath said, I will dwell in them, and walk in them; and I will be their God, and they shall be my people.

17Wherefore come out from among them, and be ye separate, saith the Lord, and touch not the unclean thing; and I will receive you.

18And will be a Father unto you, and ye shall be my sons and daughters, saith the Lord Almighty".

Again we see that we are not to have fellowship with the kingdom of darkness because what has light, which is the Kingdom of God, got to with darkness? I am not saying that we cut relationship with those who do not yet believe and accept Jesus Christ as their savior and Lord. Jesus sat with sinners because he had love for them. He came to seek and save the lost. The relationship I am talking about is the relationship with the devil in terms of feasting and drinking from his table. However, if the relationship you have with the unbelievers is taking you back into the kingdom of darkness, and to what is unclean, then you need to come out from among them. Come out so that you do not become defiled again! Come out so that your souls are preserved for the heavenly kingdom!

So now, what about feasting and drinking from the table of God's kingdom? Jesus said in John 6:33 and 35, "For the bread of God is he which cometh down from heaven, and giveth life unto the world ... I am the bread of life: he that cometh to me shall never hunger; and he that believeth on me shall never thirst". The bread of God is His Word. The temptation in Matthew 4:4, Jesus said, "It is written, Man shall not live by bread alone, but by every word that proceedeth out of the mouth of God". Jesus is referred to the Word in John 1:14; "And the Word was made flesh, and dwelt among us, (and we beheld his glory, the glory as of the only begotten of the Father,) full of grace and truth".

In contrast, we see that from the kingdom of darkness comes the "bread of affliction; water of affliction" (I Kings 22:27). This is the account where King Ahab, angry with the prophecy of prophet Micaiah, told his servants to throw the prophet in prison and feed him thus. Jesus is the bread of life and when we eat of His table, we shall never hunger. But if we feast at the table of darkness we get the bread of affliction. When we drink at the table of Jesus, we shall never thirst. John 4:13-14 Jesus speaks of himself as the living waters, "Jesus answered and said unto her, Whosoever drinketh of this water shall thirst again: But whosoever drinketh of the water that I shall give him shall never thirst; but the water that I shall give him shall be in him a well of water springing up into everlasting life". But when we drink from the kingdom of darkness we drink the water of afflictions.

Our souls can only be satisfied at the table of God's Kingdom. The vacuum in our souls will be filled. There is a contentment that nothing in the world could give but the food and water that is served at the table of the Kingdom of God's dear Son of love. If we feast frequently at the table of the Kingdom of God's Son of love, we will acquire godly characteristics. We will bear or manifest the fruit of the Spirit which is, according to Galatians 5, "… love, joy, peace, longsuffering, gentleness, goodness, faith, Meekness, temperance: against such there is no law." Notice that the fruit described here is singular – fruit not fruits. That means all the manifestation of the fruit of the Spirit is what we are to bear. We cannot pick and choose. We cannot say I have peace and faith and excuse ourselves of the weakness of patience or longsuffering. There are other fruits that scripture mentions. "By him therefore let us offer the sacrifice of praise to God continually, that is, the fruit of our lips giving thanks to his name" (Hebrews 13:15). Fruit of giving thanks not complaining. It expresses a praise note of gratitude and being positive not negative. "Bring forth therefore fruits meet for repentance" (Matthew 3:8)". If we keep going back to feast and drink from the kingdom of darkness, there is no true fruits of repentance. "Being filled with the fruits of righteousness, which are by Jesus Christ, unto the glory and praise of God" (Philippians 1:11). Feasting and drinking from the kingdom of darkness will not bring you fruits of righteousness. "But the wisdom that is from above is first pure, then peaceable, gentle, and easy to be intreated, full of mercy and good fruits, without partiality, and without hypocrisy" (James 3:17). When we continually feast and drink from the table of kingdom of God's own Son of love, we become more and more like Jesus.

How much fruit we produce or how much fruit is multiplied in our lives and in the lives of others depend on how much we frequent the table of the Lord and how much time we spend in the chamber of the Lord. The parable of the sower and the seeds shows the varying degree of the return on the seed of God's word planted in a person's heart or life. Some were able to reproduce 30 fold, some 60 and others 100. But yet for some there was none because they allow the devil to take the word from them immediately with doubts and unbelief. Others who are not rooted deep enough, wither away from the word because of tribulation and persecution. Still others allow riches and cares of this world to choke the word out and therefore were unfruitful. Where do you stand in the reproduction of God's word in your life and in others? That would be a clue if you have been feasting and drinking from the kingdom of darkness or the Kingdom of God.

John 15:1-8 gives us the idea of a sort of continuity of bearing fruit: "... bear fruit ... bear more fruit ... bear much fruit." Since you accepted Christ as your savior and Lord have you seen a progression in bearing fruits of the Kingdom of God? Has it progressed, digressed or is fruit bearing stagnant? In God's kingdom it is progress. Stagnancy and digression do not describe God's kingdom because we are to move from glory to glory. Jesus said in John 15 that if we abide in Him (that goes to say if we feast and drink from his table), we will bear fruit and continue to bear fruit of the Kingdom of God.

Smith Wigglesworth said that "we will never know the mind of God until we learn to know the voice of God". Feasting and drinking from the table of the kingdom of darkness will not cause us to hear the voice of God. If we think we can feast and drink from the table of the Kingdom of God and from the table of the kingdom of darkness, we are deceived. We cannot hear God's voice clearly because the "voice of the stranger" from the kingdom of darkness is pressing hard on us because we have feasted and drunk at the devil's table. If we cannot hear God's voice clearly, then we will find it hard to know His will for us. And surely we will not bear the fruit of God's Kingdom. **A true citizen**

of heaven therefore, feasts and drinks at the table of the Kingdom of God.

Chapter 8

A True Citizen of Heaven
Worships God in Spirit and in Truth
(By Gordon Tan)

"But the hour is coming, and now is, when the true worshipers shall worship the Father in spirit and truth, for the Father seeks such to worship Him. God is a spirit, and they who worship Him must worship in spirit and in truth." (John 4:23-24)

True citizens of the Kingdom of God engage in kingdom worship. They are true worshippers who worship God in spirit and in truth. They are the people that the Father seeks to worship Him.

<u>What is Kingdom Worship?</u>

When Jesus began His ministry on earth, He proclaimed the preaching of His forerunner, John the Baptist: **"Repent, for the kingdom of heaven is at hand!" (Matt 4:17)** Jesus' mission was to re-establish the kingdom of heaven here on earth that was lost via Adam's sin to the prince of this world, Satan. Just before He began His ministry, Jesus was baptized by John and was led to the wilderness by the Spirit where He fasted forty days and forty nights and was tempted by the devil. The devil made three attempts at Jesus. At the third and final attempt, the devil offered Jesus a shortcut to restoring the kingdom of heaven. He offered Jesus the kingdoms of the world if Jesus would only fall down and worship him! Jesus' reply was **"You shall worship the LORD your God and Him only you shall serve" (Matthew 4:10)**

Therefore, in order to re-establish the kingdom of heaven, Jesus had to re-establish kingdom worship here on earth among the people who would put their trust in Him for salvation. In his first attempt, Satan knew Jesus was hungry and he tempted Him to use His supernatural powers to turn stone into bread. Jesus' answer was: **It is written, Man shall not live by bread alone, but by every word that proceeds out of the mouth of God." (Matthew 4:4***)* His actions must be based on the absolute truth of the Word of God, not situational truths like "I am hungry, and so I can do whatever it takes to get food".

In his second attempt, Satan asked Jesus to cast Himself down from a pinnacle of the Temple – he even quoted scripture and attempted to misapply the Truth. But Jesus responded: **It is written again, "You shall not tempt the Lord your God." (John 4:7)** This means that you must not test or tempt the Spirit of God – even if there is apparently scripture to support your actions, it must still be in line with the Holy Spirit.

What are the basic meanings of "worship", "worship in spirit" and "worship in truth"? How do they relate to the Word of God and the Holy Spirit?

What is "worship"?

The simplest meaning of worship is related to the word "worth-ship". It is attributing worth to an object such as to give it honor, glory, love, devotion, bowing down to it, offering sacrifices to it and making sacrifices for it etc. Mankind was created for worship. It is inherent in the human nature to worship. Every person worships something in his or her life. It is in the object of worship that people differ. To determine what your personal object of worship is, simply ask yourself this question: "What object do I love the most or what object do I spend the most time and energy running after?" The root object in the answer(s) that you come up with will be your personal object of worship. Is it material things? Is it money? Is it fame or your career? Is it family or friends? Is it education? Is it pleasure or leisure? Or is it God? The object of worship in the kingdom of heaven, or kingdom worship, is the Almighty God! Worship is not about music, dancing, church services, traditions, rituals or any other practice of religion. Worship is simply a lifestyle, a relationship of love. Since kingdom worship is a personal love relationship with God, then the best definition of worship in the kingdom of heaven is **"And you shall love the LORD your God with all your heart, with all your soul, with all your mind, and with all your strength." (Mark 12:30)**

When the scribe who questioned Jesus heard His response, he expressed his agreement and understanding of what Jesus said. (Mark 12:32-33) Then, when Jesus saw that he answered wisely, said that he was **"not far from the kingdom of God"! (Mark 12:34)** This is then very close to the definition of worship – kingdom worship. What is missing? Since God is Spirit, true worshippers must worship in spirit. (John 4:24)

What is "worship in spirit"?

Why does the "worship" defined above not include the spirit? All the components in the Mark 12:30 (heart, soul, mind, strength) refer to the soulish, carnal man – the flesh! Before the fall, Adam and Eve enjoyed a perfect spirit to Spirit relationship with God. Their natural man (flesh) was in submission to their spiritual man. They fell into sin when they made a decision to use their reasoning (flesh) to justify eating the fruit from the tree of the knowledge of good and evil – in defiance of their spirit and their relationship with God. From that moment on, their flesh is exalted above their spirit and took control of man, breaking their original relationship with God.

Man's spirit is always ready to worship God but has been hindered by the flesh. The natural man seeks to satisfy the hunger of the spirit man for worship by worshipping idols and other objects. In order to return to the restored kingdom worship, man must submit every part of their flesh to love God! When man's flesh is once again placed under the Lordship of Christ, his spirit will become re-connected to the Spirit of God in a worship relationship! Philippians 3:3 defines "worship in spirit" this way **"For we [Christians] are the true circumcision, who worship God in spirit and by the Spirit of God and exult and glory and pride ourselves in Jesus Christ, and put no confidence or dependence [on what we are] in the flesh and on outward privileges and physical advantages and external appearances—"** (Amplified Bible)

The spirit is one of the essential ingredients that Jesus added to the definition of kingdom worship. The spirit man that worships God must be submitted to and controlled by the Holy Spirit. Without the influence of the Holy Spirit, a worshipper can be deceived and worship in "another" spirit or actually still in the flesh. **Beloved, do not believe every spirit, but try the spirits to see if they are of God, because many false prophets have gone out into the world. By this you know the Spirit of God: every spirit that confesses that Jesus Christ has come in the flesh is of God; and every spirit that does not confess that Jesus Christ has come in the flesh is not of God. (1-John 4:1-3)**

What then is the other ingredient that tries the spirits and eliminates deception in worship? True worshippers must also worship in truth.

What is "worship in truth"?

One aspect of "worship in truth" is to worship God truthfully, honestly, with integrity and to be "real", in other words, offering God the **"unleavened bread of sincerity and truth" (I Corinthians 5:8).** Isn't this aspect included when we worship God in spirit? Why then did Jesus add this as the third essential ingredient into kingdom worship? It is difficult to fathom that a worshipper who apparently loves God with "all your heart, with all your soul, with all your mind, and with all your strength" and worshipping honestly in apparent submission to, and controlled by the Holy Spirit can still be in deception!

The key word is "apparent". God is all knowing and therefore nothing can be hidden from Him. However, the church and the people of God are not and can still be deceived – especially in these last days! **Know this also, that in the last days grievous times will be at hand. For men will be self-lovers, money-lovers, boasters, proud, blasphemers, disobedient to parents, unthankful, unholy, without natural affection, unyielding, false accusers, without self-control, savage, despisers of good, traitors, reckless, puffed up, lovers of pleasure rather than lovers of God, <u>having a form of godliness, but denying the power of it</u>. (II Timothy 3:1-5)**

Satan, the great deceiver, is at work even more than before. Although he knows that he has been defeated by Jesus' death and resurrection, he knows that people, including Christians, still have the freedom to choose whom they would serve. According to Jesus in Matthew 4:10, worship is the perquisite to service. Therefore if Satan can create deceptions in the worship of the church today, he will be able to draw many away from kingdom worship and to serve the alternate master to God – "mammon"! **"No one can serve two masters. For** either he will hate the one and love the other, or else he will hold to the one and despise the other. You cannot serve God and mammon." (Matthew 6:24)

The word "mammon" has been translated as money, wealth or riches. We have often associated it with materialism. In the context of worship, it is better understood as "commercialism". There is a high degree of commercialization in the churches today with hi-tech equipment, TV broadcasts and Internet webcasts. Professionals are hired to play musical instruments and even to "lead worship" so that the church can achieve a "commercial" standard. Every ministry that one can dream of is set up to cater for the needs of the people. Service style and worship style is tailored or "purpose-driven" to suit the cultural profile of the community. It is good for churches to explore the use of modern technology, but not to such an extent as to compromise the anointing of God!

Can we commercialize the anointing? Are we really worshipping and serving God in these projects? Or are we packaging God to appeal to our customers (commercialization)? Are we making idols – gods after the heart of the market? **"For the time is coming when people will not endure sound teaching, but having itching ears they will accumulate for themselves teachers to suit their own passions, and will turn away from listening to the truth and wander off into myths."** (II Timothy 4:3-4)

Often church visitors do not return because the church lacked the functionality they needed e.g. nursery or children's church. True citizens of heaven would pray and seek God to determine when He wants them to go and what He wants them to contribute to that local body of Christ. One can "worship in truth" and yet can still be in error and deceived if the truth is compromised. Therefore, "worship in truth" must also be worship in light of the absolute truth of the Word of God. **"Your Word is a lamp to my feet, and a light to my path." (Psalm 119:105)**

Hebrews 4:12 says **"For the Word of God is living and powerful and sharper than any two-edged sword, piercing even to the dividing apart of soul and spirit, and of the joints and marrow, and is a discerner of the thoughts and intents of the heart."** The critical role of the Word of God in worship is to guide the worshipper to worship in truth and according to the Truth (absolute truth). The Word divides what is of the soul and what is of the spirit of the worship by discerning the thoughts and intents of the heart. Without the Word, there is no division between the soul and the spirit resulting in a worship that is performance based, soulish and variable in truth.

<u>In Summary</u>

A true citizen of heaven is a kingdom (true) worshipper who seeks to please God at all costs without compromise. As true citizens of heaven, Kingdom worship is our lifestyle and this worship is characterized by:
- An extreme love for God in everything we do, say or think – all our hearts, souls, minds, and strength.
- A worship that is in spirit. Our spirit man ruling our flesh and is "in-tune" to the leading of the Holy Spirit
- A worship that is in truth, purified by the light of the Word of God.

PART 3 DIVINE CONNECTION

Chapter 9

A True Citizen of Heaven Abides in the Vine

John 15:1-8

[1] "I am the true vine, and My Father is the vinedresser.
[2] Every branch in Me that does not bear fruit He takes away; and every *branch* that bears fruit He prunes, that it may bear more fruit.
[3] You are already clean because of the word which I have spoken to you.
[4] Abide in Me, and I in you. As the branch cannot bear fruit of itself, unless it abides in the vine, neither can you, unless you abide in Me.
[5] "I am the vine, you *are* the branches. He who abides in Me, and I in him, bears much fruit; for without Me you can do nothing.
[6] If anyone does not abide in Me, he is cast out as a branch and is withered; and they gather them and throw *them* into the fire, and they are burned.
[7] If you abide in Me, and My words abide in you, you will ask what you desire, and it shall be done for you.

[8] By this My Father is glorified, that you bear much fruit; so you will be My disciples.

In chapter 3 I mentioned that as a covenant people, the church, who is the body of Christ; *must live, move and have our being* in Jesus who is the head (Acts 17:28). Only as we do that we can bear the fruit that God expects us to bear. It is clear from scripture that there are different fruits that an individual can bear. The kind of fruits we bear says a lot about whether we are abiding in the vine or not. Matthew 7:17-20 state, "[17]Even so every good tree bringeth forth good fruit; but a corrupt tree bringeth forth evil fruit. [18]A good tree cannot bring forth evil fruit, neither can a corrupt tree bring forth good fruit. [19]Every tree that bringeth not forth good fruit is hewn down, and cast into the fire. [20]Wherefore by their fruits ye shall know them."

The Branch Draws Life from the Vine

The branch draws its life, its nutrition and even its literal physical support from the main vine. We must draw our life: our spiritual food and drink from Jesus. Jesus said that He is the bread of life and those who come to Him for drink will never thirst again. "And Jesus said unto them, I am the bread of life: he that cometh to me shall never hunger; and he that believeth on me shall never thirst (John 6:35)." "But whosoever drinketh of the water that I shall give him shall never thirst; but the water that I shall give him shall be in him a well of water springing up into everlasting life (John 4:14)."

The main channel for an individual to partake of physical food and drink is through the mouth. However, spiritual food can be received through two main channels: the eye gate and the ear gate. What we see and what we hear adds on as food and drink in our lives. This spiritual food and drink can be either from the kingdom of darkness or the Kingdom of God. I have discussed this subject in length in chapter 7.

The Branch Bears Fruit Abiding in the Vine

The point I am trying to convey here is that in order to bear the fruit that God wants, we have to abide in the vine, Jesus. If we are not abiding in Jesus, we are abiding in other trees and the fruit we bear is not the fruit of God but the fruit of something else. It could be the fruit of the kingdom of darkness or the fruit of our self-centeredness.

The passage in the beginning states that the branch cannot bear fruit by itself. It goes on to say that without Jesus, the Vine, we can do nothing. We cannot go in and out of our relationship with Jesus and expect to continue to bear the fruit of God. No branch when cut off from the main tree or vine can survive by itself, least of all, bear fruit. Neither can we go in and out of our relationship with Jesus and expect our fruit to remain. A branch with fruits when it is cut off from the main tree, the fruits will fall off because it does not have the main tree to sustain them.

Many of us frequently go in and out of our relationship with Jesus. If we have time for Him, we give Him some attention. If we do not have time for Him, we are busy with our own agendas and we leave Him out. If we are facing trails and we do not understand we say He does not care or do not even exist and we start drifting away from Him. In verse 2 it says that if the branch bears fruit, that branch is pruned so that it can bear more fruit. We have to keep abiding in Him no matter what the circumstances are. A branch stays on the tree or vine regardless of what season it is. A branch that is cut off from the tree is no longer part of the tree. It does not have its identity of the tree anymore.

Consequence of a Branch that does not abide

Verse 6 clearly tells us the consequence of not abiding in the vine. The branch will wither away because it does not have the essentials to live. Without a growing vital relationship with Jesus we will wither away in our spiritual life which affects our physical life and ultimately lead to spiritual death. Many believers deceive themselves when they think that once they have said the sinner's prayer and entered into a covenant relationship with God through Jesus Christ that they can go on with life doing their own thing. Every branch that is abiding in the vine keeps drawing nutrient from the vine to have its vitality. Believers have to keep drawing the essential nutrient from the vine so that it keeps growing healthy and able to bear fruit.

The other grave consequence for the branch that is not abiding in the vine and does not bear fruit is gathered together with other withered branches and thrown into the fire to be burnt. This is a grim picture of a branch being no longer useful for the kingdom of God. It is also a picture of what is going to happen to those who call themselves by the name of Lord Jesus Christ but do not abide in Him and bear fruit. Many believers for one reason or another; or one excuse or another do not see that serving the Lord is of importance. In every church we see the lack of people willing to serve. They just want to sit there and watch others do the work. The problem with many of these chair or bench warmers is that they not only sit but they complain, criticize and judge others. Jesus is not looking for converts who sits but disciples who will go and carry out the purposes of God's Kingdom. In verse 8 it says that if we abide in Jesus bearing much fruit, God will be glorified and we are His disciples. Jesus is coming back as the King of kings and the Lord of lords. If we are not loving and serving Him now, we are not ready to rule and reign with Him!

Essential Nutrient for the Branch

In verse 7 of John 15 it says that if we abide in Jesus it means that His words abide in us, as well. John 1:1 says that Jesus was with God, and that Word was God. Jesus is the living Word. God's Word should be alive in us like essential nutrients that give us health and enabling us to bear good fruit for Him. It is one thing to know God's Word and another thing to live it. Many believers can quote verses, share and teach the Word but if they do not live it, the Word of God is not alive in them. They can even perform signs, wonders and miracles but if they do not live the Word of God, the Word of God is not alive in them. The earlier passage in Matthew 7 continues with Jesus saying that even those who call Him "Lord, lord" and those who prophesy in His name, casting out demons in His name and doing many wonders in His name, He said He did not know. In fact He told them to depart from Him and called them lawless. To be called lawless means that the Word of God is not lived out in us.

However, if we abide in Jesus the Vine and in God's Words, whatever we desire and ask of the Lord, it shall be done for us. What a great promise to have. Psalm 37:4 tells us to take delight in the Lord and He shall give us the desires of our hearts. Abiding in Him shows that we are taking delight in the Lord. God wants to bless us but we have to take delight in Him because in Him is all the resources we need pertaining to this life He has given us on earth. Not to take delight in Him is like a branch cut off from the vine that has all the nutrient it needs to be a branch that is fruitful. **A true citizen of heaven abides in the Vine.**

Chapter 10

A True Citizen of Heaven Returns to Biblical Root

Romans 11:16-25

[16] For if the firstfruit be holy, the lump is also holy: and if the root be holy, so are the branches.

[17] And if some of the branches be broken off, and thou, being a wild olive tree, wert grafted in among them, and with them partakest of the root and fatness of the olive tree;

[18] Boast not against the branches. But if thou boast, thou bearest not the root, but the root thee.

[19] Thou wilt say then, The branches were broken off, that I might be grafted in.

[20] Well; because of unbelief they were broken off, and thou standest by faith. Be not highminded, but fear:

[21] For if God spared not the natural branches, take heed lest he also spare not thee.

[22] Behold therefore the goodness and severity of God: on them which fell, severity; but toward thee, goodness, if thou continue in his goodness: otherwise thou also shalt be cut off.

[23] And they also, if they abide not still in unbelief, shall be grafted in: for God is able to graft them in again.

[24] For if thou wert cut out of the olive tree which is wild by nature, and wert grafted contrary to nature into a good olive tree: how much more shall these, which be the natural branches, be grafted into their own olive tree?

[25]For I would not, brethren, that ye should be ignorant of this mystery, lest ye should be wise in your own conceits; that blindness in part is happened to Israel, until the fulness of the Gentiles be come in.

Instead of the picture of the branches abiding in the vine, we see here branches grafted into the Olive tree. The passage in Romans 11 shows that since we are being grafted to the olive tree, we draw our sap and nourishment from the same root. The Church being supported by the same root is thus planted in Hebraic soil and finds its true identity only when it is connected with its Jewish roots. Believers have no cause to be arrogant and be self-sufficient since we are very much dependent upon the Jews for our salvation and spiritual existence. We were once not a people but by the grace of God, we have become His people through Jesus Christ (I Peter 2:10). We have much to learn from God's chosen people and not dismiss them. So, to think ""Christianly" was to also think Hebraically."[1]

So, Marvin R. Wilson, through his book, <u>Our Father Abraham, Jewish Roots of the Christian Faith</u> is attempting to not only bring an awareness of the gradual departure of the church from its Jewish Roots, the problems that has arisen because of this departure but also how we can work toward the restoration of the church to its Jewish heritage.

---

[1] Our Father Abraham Jewish Roots of the Christian Faith by Marvin R. Wilson. © 1989 Our Father Abraham Jewish Roots of the Christian Faith by Marvin R. Wilson. © 1989 Wm. B. Eerdmans Publishing Company 2140 Oak Industrial Drive N.E., Grand Rapids, MI 49503 and Center for Judaic-Christian. Chapter 1 The Root and the Branches – The Olive Root and Branches Pg 12

The early gentile believers joined themselves with God's people. They adjusted to join themselves with God's people not the reverse. They even participated in the Jewish feasts. The Olive tree represents one people of God. It was never the abandoning of the ancestral Jewish faith but rather after being reconciled to God they were to be a part of the Jewish community. The early Church was viewed as a sect within Judaism. In Acts 24:5 they were seen as "the sect of the Nazarenes". "In its origin, Christianity was Jewish to the very core. The essentially non-Jewish character of today's Church is a matter of history, not a question of origins."[2]

It seems that Paul's warning in Romans 11 to the gentile believers went unheeded. The gentile believers claimed that they have replaced Israel against the teaching of Paul who taught that God did not reject his people, for the gifts and calling of God are irrevocable. By tearing itself from her Jewish roots the Church started defining itself in non-Jewish terminology. Some of the examples given by Wilson are: instead of the Hebrew 'Messiah' it became Greek Christ, the 'Messiah Jeshua' became Jesus Christ the Son of God, the 'Nazarenes' became the Christians, the 'Scriptures' became 'the Old Testament' and the 'Israel of God' became the Holy Church.[3]

It is no wonder that Wilson, in the preface cited that Christian educators for so long have been stressing "the origins, impact, and contributions of Western civilization on the Church and modern society" but often treat "the Hebrew world and the modern Jewish community of the Diaspora" as being "superficial,

---

[2] Our Father Abraham Jewish Roots of the Christian Faith by Marvin R. Wilson. © 1989 Chapter 3 The Earliest Church and Judaism – Beginnings: A Jewish Church Pg 43

[3] Our Father Abraham Jewish Roots of the Christian Faith by Marvin R. Wilson. © 1989 Chapter 7 A History of Contempt: Anti-Semitism and the Church. Pg 89

optional or even irrelevant." [4] Jesus sat under the teaching of Moses, the Torah, the Prophets and the Psalms and not under Plato and the Greco-Roman academies. Paul and all the other Apostles also taught from the Torah, the Prophets and the Psalms because they did not have the New Testament yet! Even though the New Testament was written in Greek, the Hebraic background was its very core. "The Old Testament is the foundation of the New. The message of the New Testament is in the Hebrew tradition as against the Greek tradition." [5]

By the middle of the second century the Church Fathers widened the rift between the gentile Christians and the Jews further in the antagonistic writings. The Church sought for any evidence they could find to show that Judaism was a dead legalistic religion.

Wilson gave a few guidelines on how the Church could be restored back to our Jewish roots. Earlier on in the foregoing paragraphs we saw that because of interpretations that came from a western Greco-Roman mindset and gentile mindset and little understanding of the Hebraic background, it was part of the reason why we have drifted away from our Jewish roots. The core of this misinterpretation was pertaining to scriptures. So, the first guideline Wilson offered is to restore the Old Testament to its proper place by following the attitude of Jesus and those who wrote the New Testament toward the Old Testament. They granted full authority and inspiration to the Old Testament. [6]

---

[4] Our Father Abraham Jewish Roots of the Christian Faith by Marvin R. Wilson. © 1989 Preface - pg xv
[5] Our Father Abraham Jewish Roots of the Christian Faith by Marvin R. Wilson. © 1989 Chapter 1 The Root and the Branches – Athens of Jerusalem? Pg 9
[6] Our Father Abraham Jewish Roots of the Christian Faith by Marvin R. Wilson. © 1989 Chapter 8 The Old Testament: Hebraic Foundation of the Church – The Bible of the Early Church pg 112

The second guideline is for the Church to remember that without both testaments, the Bible is incomplete and limited in value. The mistake that the early Church Fathers made concerning the Bible is to separate the Bible into Old and New Testament. Old has the implication because it is older it is either not relevant or optional. It also gives the idea of non-continuity. The third guideline is "to remember that the Old Testament is the theological key for opening the door to the New Testament".[7] The Old Testament gives the foundational understanding of many aspects of life, of creation, of relationship to God, of divine grace that brought salvation and the Kingdom of God. Without these foundational pillars we will have unbalanced teaching and even lead to heresies. Marcion taught heresies and it greatly influenced some of the Church doctrines up to the present.

The "fourth guideline is to examine carefully the issues of Old Testament authority and interpretation". Many interpreters go beyond what is the plain and literal meaning of a passage without clear biblical warrant. Wilson emphasized "that a text must be first heard on its own terms, distinct literary genre, in its own Testament." [8] He also stressed that all of the Old Testament is God-breathed and useful, even if it is genealogies and levitical laws and sacrifices. It is not a buffet table where we are free to pick and choose what we think is or is not relevant.

The fifth guideline is the need to acknowledge and affirm the Jewishness of Christ. He was born to a Jewish father and mother. He grew up in a Jewish culture and was taught the Hebraic ways of God. He ministered as Jew. The sixth guideline is the need to receive from other resources which provide Hebraic

---

[7] Chapter 8 The Old Testament: Hebraic Foundation of the Church – The Theological Key pg 113

[8] Our Father Abraham Jewish Roots of the Christian Faith by Marvin R. Wilson. © 1989 Chapter 8 The Old Testament: Hebraic Foundation of the Church – God-Breathed and Useful pg 114

April 13, 2011

Dearest Ho,

A quick note. It was such a blessing to visit with you. I'm sorry I could not send you down. That night my room mate had a problem getting into the room too with her key.

I'm sending you my book as an early Mother's Day gift. Pray that these books will go into the hands of those who call themselves Christians but they are not; to wake them up. It will be available on Amazon.com soon.
I'm praying for Pavik.

Love,
Christina

insights to both Testaments. The Church in its removal of anything of Judaism has also thrown out resources of Jewish root which actually would enrich our understanding of the Testaments. This leads us into seventh guideline and that is to rediscover the Hebraic foundation of the Church because the core of Christianity is Jewish; its life, structure and practices.[9]

The seven guidelines above deal mainly with the theological aspect of restoration of the Church back to its Jewish roots. However, the most important aspect of restoration has to be the fuel of love. The first step before one can love truly is to acknowledge our sin and repent. As Wilson pointed out, the gentile Church not only drifted away from its Jewish roots but had become arrogant, boastful and hostile causing a history of anti-Judaism and anti-Semitism. I cannot help but remember what Dwight Pryor's said, "Jesus came to die for the Jews but the Church have reversed it by making the Jews die for Jesus."

The greatest commandment that Jesus taught us is to love God with all our heart, soul and strength and to love our neighbor as ourselves. Wilson chose the right verse for the last chapter, "Let us not love with words or tongue but with actions and in truth." (I John 3:18) As His followers in our treatment to the Jews, His very own people, we fall short of being a true follower. We are not following a set of rules but we are following Jesus. Our faith in Jesus is a relationship that should overflow in our relationship with others. Our gratitude and love for Jesus should overflow in our love for others. I have always concurred with those who proclaim that Christianity is not a religion but a relationship. The definition of religion has to do with a set of beliefs governing our behavior and worship. Religion binds us to certain rites, duties,

---

[9] Chapter 8 The Old Testament: Hebraic Foundation of the Church – Christianity is Jewish pg 125

vows or obligations. That is why in so many churches where the spirit of religion takes precedent over relationship with God, it is lifeless. But even this life is not an abundant life without our Jewish root. The root of the Olive tree that supports us brings the nourishment that we need to have the abundant life in God. All others are kind of like supplements to our diet!

Even though it is going to be a long road to reverse the damage done when the Church, as a grafted branch, pulled away from its Hebraic or biblical roots, it has to start now not later. The Church has to wake up and recognize this deep problem now not later lest what Paul warns in Romans11:21-24 befalls the Church. Additionally, the Church needs to wake up now because she will not be ready when Jesus, the Bridegroom comes. The bride was given specific instructions in order to be ready while the bridegroom is away at this time preparing a place for His bride. The Bridegroom will only receive those who have followed those instructions to be ready and those instructions are in the Hebraic teachings. Revelation 19:7 (NKJV) states, "… and His wife has made herself ready."From the time we are born again of the Holy Spirit to the time when Jesus is coming again, it is time to get ourselves ready according to the specific instructions the Bridegroom left behind for us to follow. **A true citizen of heaven returns to biblical root.**

Covenant Prayer

The God of Abraham, Isaac and Jacob, thank you for making a way to reconcile me to You through Jesus Christ (Yeshua). Thank you for sending Jesus to die and shed His blood on the cross for my sin and that He rose again that I too might have life and life eternal. I acknowledge that I have sinned against you and thus have been separated from you. I accept Jesus as my Savior and Lord. Please forgive me and cleanse me from all unrighteousness. I thank You that as I do so, You send Your Holy Spirit as a seal upon me. Just as Abraham accepted Your covenant, I accept Your covenant through the shed blood of Jesus Messiah. Help me, by Your Holy Spirit to grow in this new life with You.

In Jesus' most precious name, Amen.

BIBLIOGRAPHY

Our Father Abraham Jewish Roots of the Christian Faith by Marvin R. Wilson. © 1989 Wm. B. Eerdmans Publishing Company 2140 Oak Industrial Drive N.E., Grand Rapids, MI 49503 and Center for Judaic-Christian.

Preface - Pg xv
Chapter 1 The Root and the Branches – Athens of Jerusalem? Pg 9
Chapter 1 The Root and the Branches – The Olive Root and Branches. Pg 12
Chapter 3 The Earliest Church and Judaism – Beginnings: A Jewish Church. Pg 43
Chapter 7 A History of Contempt: Anti-Semitism and the Church. Pg 89
Chapter 8 The Old Testament: Hebraic Foundation of the Church – The Bible of the Early Church. Pg 112
Chapter 8 The Old Testament: Hebraic Foundation of the Church – The Theological Key. Pg 113
Chapter 8 The Old Testament: Hebraic Foundation of the Church – God-Breathed and Useful. Pg 114
Chapter 8 The Old Testament: Hebraic Foundation of the Church – Christianity is Jewish. Pg 125

About the Author

R. C. Lee is a licensed minister with an international ministerial organization, as well as, a licensed minister in her church group that has over 3,000 churches worldwide.

She has been in ministry for over 30 years. She and her husband have been working across denominational line with many pastors and church leaders. They have three children who are also in ministry with them.